Fr. Enrique L

MOTHER AGREDA
AND THE
MARIOLOGY OF VATICAN II

Translated by Fr. Peter Damian Fehlner, FI

FRANCISCANS OF
STOKE
THE IMMACULATE

Academy of the Immaculate
New Bedford, MA

Mother Agreda And The Mariology Of Vatican II, is a new, unabridged translation of the original Spanish edition: *La Madre Agreda y la Mariología del Vaticano II* (Salamanca 2003).

This is book prepared for publication by the Franciscans of the Immaculate [marymediatrix.com], POB 3003, New Bedford, MA, 02741-3003.

Cum Permissu Superiorum

ISBN: 978-1-60114-042-5

MOTHER AGREDA
AND THE
MARIOLOGY OF VATICAN II

By Fr. Enrique Llamas, OCD

CONTENTS

FOREWORD

Writing this foreword to the essay of Fr. Enrique Llamas, OCD, on Mother Agreda and the mariology of Vatican II has been for me a source of great satisfaction.

His study is one of the praiseworthy fruits of multiple activities and projects carried out in connection with the fourth centenary celebrations of the birth of Sister Mary of Jesus of Agreda (1602-2002). Among the many objectives stressed in this commemoration, most prominent are those of making the figure and work of this great woman better known, and above all, with greater commitment and interest, of bringing the cause of her beatification still pending before the Sacred Congregation for the Causes of Saints to a happy conclusion.

On completion of the work of its Theological Study Commission, the Sacred Congregation for the Doctrine of the Faith, through the Vatican Secretariat of State, released an official commentary. This commentary, while seconding the conclusion of the study commission, viz., that one may not claim as present in the *Mystical City of God* doctrinal errors or heresies in any genuine sense of those terms, nonetheless the Congregation for the Doctrine of the Faith believes the figure of the Mother of God, as it is set out in this work, *conflicts* with that found in Sacred Scripture and *is not compatible* with the mariology set forth by Vatican II. This commentary concludes, nonetheless, that while admitting the positive fruits of recent study, the Congregation for the Doctrine of the Faith has decided not to grant the *nihil obstat* required for a continuation of the process of beatification. The reason is that any continuation of the Cause would carry with it an implicit approbation of a seriously dubious book and constitute an indirect promotion of the book itself. The document is dated Rome, February 19, 1999.

From the above-cited reply it is clear that the question of the *nihil obstat* has not been definitively resolved, but remains open to revision on the basis of new studies and further reflections.

This study of Fr. Llamas, OCD, President of the Spanish Mariological Society, Professor emeritus of the Pontifical University of Salamanca, and one of the foremost experts in mariology, is a very valuable contribution and a strong witness to the theme which concerns us who admire this great nun. For it offers rigorous and conclusive arguments for resolving the difficulties blocking the continuation of the process for the cause of beatification of Mother Agreda.

The work we are presenting consists of two parts. The first by way of summary synthesis outlines the "biblical image" of Mary in the *Mystical City of God*. This summary illustrates how Sr. Mary of Jesus interprets texts of Sacred Scripture in a theological-spiritual key, in the context of the history of salvation and by the light of Catholic doctrine common to the authors and spiritual masters of her time. Fr. Llamas concludes that the image of the Mother of God presented to us by the *Mystical City of God*, in its fundamentals, is not *in contrast* with the image we find in Sacred Scripture.

The second and longer part is given over to a demonstration of the *compatibility* of the mariology of the *Mystical City of God* with the teaching of Vatican II. The author accomplishes this in two complementary sections. In the first section he analyses texts illustrating the full conformity of this work with the mariology of Vatican II. The presentation, in parallel columns, of the coincidence between the two, both in the doctrinal content and terminology, pedagogically renders the clarification of the disputed point very persuasive. Particularly significant is the passage treating of the active and objective, not merely passive and subjective, collaboration of the Virgin Mary in the work of Redemption in Sr. Mary of Jesus and in Vatican II (cf. *Mystical City of God*, Part II, Book III, ch. 12, no. 151; and Vatican II, *Lumen Gentium*, 61).

Secondly, Fr. Llamas proves that in the mariological teaching of Mother Agreda there are found, indeed perfected, the "notes" characteristic of true devotion to the Virgin, those signaled by Paul VI in the apostolic exhortation *Marialis Cultus:* the Trinitarian, Christological and Ecclesial (cf. *Marialis Cultus* 25-28). The author concludes that in its fundamentals the mariology of the *Mystical City of God* is fully compatible with that elaborated by Vatican II.

In addition to this there is another interesting observation and brief comment to be made as regards the marian doctrine of Vatican II. No one would even so much as question the total correspondence between the teaching of the Popes on the Virgin Mary, in particular that of Paul VI and John Paul II who lived during the Council, and the mariology and thought patterns of Vatican II.

In this context the author underscores a revealing coincidence, not to say fundamental identity of thought between the contemporary Papal Magisterium and the Ven. Mother Agreda, in her fruit of a "happy" intuition, concerning the role of Mary in the mission and function of the Apostles and in the Church beginning with the Resurrection of Jesus Christ, with His Ascension to heaven, and with Pentecost: the role of Mother and of Teacher.

Paul VI taught this in a number of documents. John Paul II has recalled this in presenting the Virgin Mary under this aspect in recently published documents. In brief, this Pope says that "the first of the signs worked by Jesus...shows us Mary precisely as Teacher...who exercised just this role with the disciples after the Ascension of Jesus, when she joined with them in awaiting the Holy Spirit." (*The Rosary of the Virgin Mary*, n. 14) Mother Agreda makes the same, identical presentation of the figure and mission of the Virgin Mary in the Church during the last period of her life.

In concluding, I would like to extend my respectful thanks to Fr. Llamas for his intense and generous dedication over many years to the study of mariology in general and the work of Mother Agreda in particular. I believe that his insights into the mariological doctrine of the Ven. Sr. Mary of Jesus on a number of themes are definitive. These themes include the predestination of Mary, the concept and significance of the virginal maternity, the effective collaboration of the Virgin Mary with her Son in the work of Redemption.

It is my heartfelt hope that Fr. Llamas' essay may be a means of clarification and a pillar of conviction in resolving difficulties and overcoming obstacles currently blocking progress in the laborious work of advancing the cause of beatification of the Ven. Mother Agreda.

May the life and work and timeless message of this important woman help all of us to enkindle the flame of hope in this hour of the world and of the Church, the dawn of the third millennium, as Pope John Paul II taught us.

Vincent Jimenez Zamora
Vicar General of the Diocese of Osma-Soria (Spain)

TRANSLATOR'S NOTE

The author of this remarkable defense, not only of the sanctity, but of the deep and accurate theological understanding of the Ven. Mary of Jesus of Agreda, author of the well-known and highly esteemed *Mystical City of God*, is well nigh unknown in the English speaking world. Fr. Enrique Llamas, OCD, in fact, is one of the leading mariologists, not only of present day Spain, but also of the Catholic Church. He is also an expert on *The Mystical City of God*. That he should add his name to the chorus of scholars who for over three hundred years have risked their reputations to defend the merits of this work, by itself, signals the importance of this study for the Church today.

Those who might desire additional information in English about the subject of this essay may find the essentials in the introductions to the four volumes of the standard English translation of Mother Agreda's renowned life of the Mother of God. The comments of Fr. George J. Blatter (penname Fiscar Marison), the translator, on the major objections to this work since its first publication in Spanish in 1670: namely the sanctity of the authoress, authenticity of her mystical experiences (e.g., the famous bi-locations to New Mexico and Texas where she converted innumerable Indian tribes before the arrival of missionaries), of her authorship of this work, and indeed the orthodoxy of the work, are amazingly perceptive and accurate for an introduction composed nearly a century ago.

To assist the reader in following Fr. Llamas' references to the Spanish critical edition, I have indicated in brackets after his reference, the volume and page (and sometimes of the paragraph number when it differs from the one volume Spanish critical edition) of the English edition (first published in 1912 in four volumes, reprinted in 1949, and again in 1971).

The work itself, as composed by the holy Authoress, comprises 8 books, arranged in three parts: part 1 (books one and two); part 2 (books three, four, five and six); part 3 (books seven and eight). The three parts are respectively entitled, *Conception; Incarnation and Transfixion; Coronation.* This arrangement is already an indication of a profound grasp of mariology, rarely matched in any other similar work. In the English translation the second part was printed in two volumes, the second volume containing books three and four, and the third, books five and six.

Most of the bibliography cited by Fr. Llamas (only a selection of what is available in Spanish) is not available in English. This is because so little interest has been taken in this work or its authoress by English speaking theologians and scholars, except on rare occasion to criticize it on the basis of accusations long since proven to be fraudulent. The ordinary faithful, some candidates for beatification, like the Ven. Solanus Casey and soon to be beatified, Ven. Antonio Margil, have not only read it, but also promoted it. In those few instances where English translations of scholarly studies exist, they have been indicated in brackets.

Elsewhere in the notes, with the approval of Fr. Llamas, I have added brief additional information or comment helpful to the English reader in contextualizing the case in favor of Mother Agreda. These additions are also bracketed.

Fr. Peter M. Fehlner, FI

PART ONE:

GENERAL INTRODUCTION

1. THE *MYSTICAL CITY OF GOD*, FRUIT OF CONTEMPLATIVE PRAYER

a) I confess to beginning this study with a profound sense of "reverential fear." Given the importance and greatness of the *Mystical City of God* (abbreviated *MCG*) [1] as a work of theology and essay illustrating a "narrative mariology," little cultivated since her time, I could not begin otherwise. This is a work born of intense interior life and singular experiences. Its object is eternal life, the mystery of God and Jesus Christ Redeemer, virginal Son of the Immaculate Virgin (cf. Jn 17:3), mysteries which transcend the range of ordinary historical knowledge and other criteria of evaluation. This fact commands respect.

D. Marcelino Menéndez Pelayo, sensing the overwhelming power of the wisdom enthralling him – and precisely for this reason – experienced "religious fright" in contacting – "touching" he said – the canticles and poetry of St. John of the Cross, so "divinely" written; a poetry "so elegant and so exquisite in form, and among the finest fruits of the renaissance, so realistic and descriptive;" [2] a poetry,

---

1 Hilda Graef, an historian of mariology, as a kind of appendix to the errors and equivocations which she commits in regard to Mother Agreda, grudgingly admits that the *MCG* is a *monumental work*, even if she considers it "unbalanced" (HILDA GRAEF, *María. La mariología y el culto mariano a través de la historia* (translated from the German), Barcelona 1968, p. 392. [English version: *Mary. A History of Doctrine and Devotion*. London 1963-1965, 2 vols.: here vol. 2, pp. 53-55. For a more sympathetic estimate in English cf. M. O'CARROLL, *Theotokos*, Wilmington DE 1983, pp. 235-236.])

2 M. MENÉNDEZ PELAYO, *Estudios y Discursos de crítica histórica y literaria*, vol. III, Madrid 1941, p. 27.

whose rhythm and beauty transport us to the realm of the ineffable.

Each time I make contact with the work of Mother Agreda I experience something similar. I am not sure I am capable of interpreting this work with full objectivity, given its unique characteristics. [3] Mother Agreda offers us a narrative mariology, an interpretation of the history of the Virgin Mary, the Immaculate Virgin, the Mother of the Son of God, collaborator with Him in the work of Redemption.

Its "elegant," yet "so exquisite" form, and its "figurative" and "realistic descriptions," for all its baroque exuberance, are the covering hiding precious pearls and jewels, the mariological truths of the Church's faith, and for that reason shade an abyss of light to our sight. But even more than this the fact that her mariology is for the most part fruit of her contemplative prayer and of her intense interior life linked to mystical experiences of the highest order, inspires in me even greater "reverential fear."

It is not possible to place oneself on the same level as the Venerable Authoress, nor match her depth of comprehension in experiencing the mysteries of faith; nor can we enter the temple of these ineffable experiences. This would surely be necessary to resolve many of the problems arising in connection with the interpretation and evaluation of the *Mystical City of God*.

---

3 Today it is generally presupposed that the *MCG* is the fruit of meditation on the mysteries of the Mother of Jesus and of contemplative prayer, rather than of academic study, in the same way as the *Mansions of the Interior Castle* of St. Teresa of Jesus are. The *Qualificatores* (examiners; investigators) of the Inquisition, finding no grounds to suspect anything amiss in the *MCG*, declared and acknowledged in 1650 that Sr. Mary of Jesus was a woman most learned in "Sacred Scripture and had attained such knowledge *more by prayer and contemplation than by study.*" Because they did not grasp this crucial point, the accusers and enemies of the *MCG* during the 17th and 18th centuries were guilty of serious misjudgments.

By way of orientation I intend to explain here the thrust and content of the mariology of the *MCG*, in order to make, not a comparison, but a simple correlation with the principles and content of the mariology of Vatican II. The distance of three centuries is no obstacle to obtaining positive results, because to obtain such, nothing else is needed from the doctrinal point of view than an analysis and application of the common principles of mariological doctrine.

The *MCG* is not an easy book to read. It is the fruit of a profound interior life and of a high contemplation of the mysteries of the Trinity and of the Incarnation, of the place of the All Holy Virgin in the saving designs of God, etc.

The explanations of its ample content are on occasion given in the form of metaphor or via interpretation of symbols, or as accounts of intellectual and imaginary visions, and of phenomena radiating from the mystery.

The fundamental content of the work is not a history, nor is it a collection or source book of dates. It is a doctrinal exposition. It is the explanation of a life: the life of the Virgin Mary, of the Mother of the Son of God, who at the same time was collaborator with Him in the work of redemption. It is an explanation based not so much on signs and exterior manifestations as on the interior reality of that Mother's privileged and singular existence, and on the life of her heart, ever nourished by a most ineffable love. For this reason we are dealing with a theology, and in great part with a "mystical theology" born of the light of faith and of the warmth of the *flame of divine love*, that flame about which St. John of the Cross sang so marvelously.

b) Mother Agreda lived in an age when mariology in Spain had reached its highest peaks and most dazzling achievements: the 17th century, golden age of Spanish mariology.

In addition to exceptional personal endowments attested by the data of her biography and acknowledged by historical scholarship, she had benefited from informed lectures and instructions on the Virgin Mary by her confessors and other Franciscan religious, just as had the other members of her cloistered Community. Further, she had also read a number of books and treatises on marian themes, and was adequately informed on a variety of theories and approaches characteristic of different theological schools of her day.

Apart from this I presuppose here – because it is the truth – that she received much more understanding of mariological truths from another source: by way of and through the exercise of meditation and contemplative prayer. She attained a *sapiential knowledge* of the mystery of Mary, as souls attain this via contemplation, of the kind St. John of the Cross speaks in his *Spiritual Canticle*, and St. Teresa of Jesus in her *Mansions of the Interior Castle*.

This becomes so perfectly clear and so perfectly certain to anyone who reads the *MCG* objectively and without prejudice, that it constitutes the principle of enlightenment and interpretative key guaranteeing the correctness of whatever the Venerable Authoress teaches from a doctrinal point of view.

c) Mother Agreda wrote many pages of her great work while listening interiorly to the Word of God or to the Virgin Mary. During contemplative prayer she came to understand what she was obliged to say. On occasion, according to her own testimony – repeated often – the Virgin Herself ordered her to put in writing what she was being taught. In view of the high knowledge she had attained of the mystery of the Mother of God, she felt a strong impulse to make this known to others.

We are not, however, dealing here with a hearing of words in the formal sense or with hearing articulated sounds. Even less are we dealing with a formal or express command – with the exception of a few rare instances. Rather, what is involved is an interior sentiment experienced in moments of contemplative prayer, experienced while reflecting on how many souls might profit as much from reading about the mysteries of the Immaculate Virgin as Mother Agreda had in perceiving them. This is a sentiment connatural to souls who are blessed with profound mystical experiences. St. Teresa, in another style and in relation to a different proposal, tells us the same thing; but in part what she says is applicable here. [4]

I believe that the Venerable Mother for the most part composed the *MCG* as fruit of interior illuminations, which she had received during moments of her life given over to mental prayer and to loving reflection on the truths and mysteries of the Immaculate Virgin. It is quite natural that, feeling herself a spiritual daughter of the Immaculate Conception, and most devoted to this singular privilege she should attribute these illuminations to the Immaculate Virgin – sometimes also ascribing them to Jesus Christ, to God and to the Trinity, on occasion in the form of dialogue. But the words themselves were soundless; most of the time she heard them with the ear of her soul, but as distinctly as if she had heard them with her bodily ear. She experienced a phenomenon fairly similar to one experienced by St. Teresa of Jesus during that period when the Inquisition had prohibited the reading of many

---

4 St. Teresa of Jesus, *Life*, 16, 3. The Saint speaks of souls who have reached the third degree of prayer, or "third way of tending the garden." God has done her such favors, that the soul desires everyone to understand her glory to the praise of God, desires to share her joy with all.

In our case Mother Agreda, a contemplative soul, desires to share knowledge of other gifts and wonders God had accomplished in the Mother of his Son, and which Mother Agreda had come to know by prayer.

spiritual books written in the form known as *romance.* This decision caused St. Teresa great pain, because it deprived her of reading books which benefited her. She appealed to the Lord; and "the Lord said to me, literally: '*Do not fret, because I will give you a living book.*' " [5]

This knowledge is attained in and received from the Spirit, when the soul reflects on the faith which works through charity, about which St. Paul speaks (cf. Gal 5:6), a reflection, therefore, activated by love. It is fruit of meditative and contemplative prayer, in so far as the intellect is not subject to the laws governing the natural mode of knowing, but rather receives both light and understanding according to the dispositions of the will in loving.

The style used by Mother Agreda in writing the *MCG* may be considered in itself as a literary genre, appropriate and adequate for a work on marian theology written by an authoress who is not a professional theologian. That notwithstanding, this work is a genuine mariology. For its contents are purely theological and spiritual rather than facts of history as such.

The Venerable Mother did not have a theological formation of the scholastic type. For that reason she could not write or compose a work of theological character on the basis of concepts or thematic expositions as this is done in scholastic treatises of mariology. It would have been extremely difficult for her to follow this method, or match the systematization generally cultivated by theologians of the school. She opted instead to follow other methods and

---

5 St. Teresa of Jesus, *Life*, 26, 6. The sorrow of the Saint consisted in this, that she was only permitted to read books in Latin which she did not understand. The classic style with few embellishments, typical of mid-16th century, reports exclusively what the Lord actually said. Mother Agreda, writing in the baroque age, embellishes and amplifies the words and phrases to express the interior locutions, embellishments not lacking in literary beauty.

employ other styles, as did St. Teresa in her book on *The Mansions*, included in her commentary on *The Canticle of Canticles:* the way of experience. In her *MCG*, in many passages, Mother Agreda talks of and expounds numerous questions on the basis of her extraordinary experiences.

In this case, the methodology most accessible to her and most appropriate for her project: viz., for the doctrinal development and explanation of the mysteries or events in the life of the Mother of Jesus, was to follow a chronological order, and so make known to others what she herself had learned by way of contemplative prayer.

Mother Agreda, therefore, had at her disposition an ample and precise theological knowledge in relation to the principal problems of mariology, a knowledge acquired in various ways: reading, conversations, listening to conferences and sermons, etc. What she surely did not possess, however, were the academic techniques and methods usually appropriate in composing an adequate exposition of all that she knew about the mystery of the Immaculate Virgin, collaborator in the work of Redemption.

This explains why she followed another method in her exposition, adopting the style of colloquy, characteristic of mental prayer. She set forth what she had learned in this way, in the same form in which the Virgin Mary, or Jesus Christ or the Trinity had revealed it to her.

Here knowledge acquired naturally via the daily reading of books and conversations with learned and devout men fuses with that sublime knowledge attained in discursive meditation and via loving contemplation of the mysteries of Jesus Christ and Mary Most Holy. It would not at all be easy to label each part and separate it from the others so as to identify what is the fruit of ordinary, contemporary erudition and what has its origin in an interior illumination, fruit of contemplation and of the action of the gifts of the Holy Spirit. There is no doubt, however, that this fusion correctly describes the circumstances and interior state in which Mother Agreda composed the greater part of her work, and which in turn principally determined the particular style adopted for its composition: that of colloquy. [6]

d) I think we may identify this method of learning followed by Mother Agreda in questions of mariology with the "way of beauty," the *via pulchitudinis*, as it has been called by Pope Paul VI. In so defining it the Pope indicated how it is *"accessible to all, including simple souls,"* distinct from the "way of truth," or path generally trod by scholars and professors of theology. [7]

Great theologians and masters of the scholastic age recognize these two ways and teach the legitimacy and value of a theology and mariology of mind and heart: *mentis et cordis*. Some, however, have violently rejected this approach. The negative stance taken on this point by the famous Dominican, Melchior Cano, master of the great

---

6 No one should be surprised at the style adopted by Mother Agreda for her work. Since the middle ages spiritual authors had been employing the very same style, in greater or less proportions. To cite one example, which we will have occasion further on to examine, the Franciscan Ubertino of Casale employs this style in many places in his *Arbor Vitae*. On many occasions it is also the style of St. Teresa of Jesus. So also St. Brigit, St. Alonso de Orozco, recently canonized, and St. Teresa attribute to causes of an extraordinary kind: intellectual visions, interior locutions, etc, a great deal of knowledge acquired via contemplative prayer. It is necessary to take account of this key to the interpretation of mystical and spiritual literature. The work of Mother Agreda is a *Mystical City of God*.

7 "*How should Mary be presented adequately to the people of God, in such wise that an increase of marian devotion is fostered in them? To realize this there are two possible ways or approaches. In the first instance there is the way of truth, i.e., of biblical, historical, theological research... This is the way of the learned... But there is in addition to this another way, accessible to all, including simple souls: this is the way of beauty:*" Paul VI, *Allocution at the close of the International Mariological-Marian Congress*, Rome 1975 (AAS 64 [1975] p. 338).

theologians of the Salamanca school, is well known. Among his disciples were the Dominicans Juan de Orellana and Juan de Lorenzana of Jesus who rejected the teaching found in works of St. Teresa of Jesus, as well as those theologians who rejected the teaching of other spiritual masters of the same century.

During the 17th century the Venerable Mother Agreda fell victim to an essentially similar opposition and incomprehension on the part of some theologians who believed themselves in possession of all theological truth. This led them to interpret and condemn on scholastic criteria a hagiographical work filled with narrative theology, and in which on many occasions the authoress appealed to a teaching she had received by way of an interior and continuous communication with God. She was thus unfairly judged by the *Qualificatores* (examiners) of the tribunal of the Inquisition in Lograno.

These considerations reveal the character and the motive of the censure of a group of professors of the Faculty of Theology of the Sorbonne (Paris) in 1696. They were simply lacking in any appreciation of mystical and spiritual knowledge, and far too much under the influence of Jansenistic ideas concerning veneration and devotion to the Mother of God.

The theology of mind and heart, attempted by Contenson in the 17th century, with a distinctive kerygmatic orientation [8] and rather less emphasis on spiritual and mystical theology, did not have anything in common either with the methodology or organization of theology during that epoch. [9] The Church preoccupied at the moment with the juridical had given

---

8 V. CONTENSON, OP, *Theologia mentis et cordis, seu speculationes universae sacrae doctrinae, pietate temperatae...: Tom. II, Liber X, De Deo Conversante. Seu de oeconomia vitae, mortis et gloriae Redemptoris... Diss. VI: Mariologia.* Lugduni 1687, pp. 169-196.

9 The classic text-books on mystical-scholastic theology, like that of Fr. Joseph of the Holy Spirit, a Carmelite from Andalusia, did not see

no attention to the mysticism of St. John of the Cross and other masters of spirituality. The theologians too often were absorbed in cold and sterile speculation, wasting their energies on fruitless polemics among the theological schools, and preoccupied with thwarting the progress of currents and tendencies reflecting distinctively Protestant influences.

In such a context, made perfectly clear for us by the history of religion, what happened a century earlier to St. Teresa of Jesus, was, sadly and lamentably, repeated in the life of Mother Mary of Jesus of Agreda. The opinion of the censors and accusers of her writings prevailed, or more exactly the tribunal of the Inquisition gave ear to their uncontrolled foolishness. The root of the accusations was very similar in both cases. In the case of St. Teresa common sense eventually prevailed. Mother Agreda, however, was victim of the power and influence of certain theologians, who enslaved to an artificial academic system were simply mistaken about how to read and interpret her mariology. The error was one of perspective, stemming from intellectual myopia, in this case compounded by an anti-feminist obsession, similar to that under which Alonso de la Fuente and associates labored when censuring the books of St. Teresa of Jesus, now Doctor of the Church.

2. A BOOK DIFFICULT TO READ AND INTERPRET: CENSURES AND ACCUSATIONS

a) It is essential, not to say absolutely necessary, to keep in mind these principles and these events, and that from the start the reader of the *MCG* adopt a position enabling him to keep the work in proper perspective: the only vantage point

---

publication until well into the 18th century. So, too, other works of spiritual theology, mainly didactic in character.

from which he can read objectively, in the proper light, the pages of this work. Its history demonstrates clearly how the errors, which suspicious readers discovered within it, and censured with disproportionate rigor and harshness, were directly consequent on the fallacy of attempting to interpret a work as singular as the *MCG* outside its context, ignoring its hagiographical style and its distinctive features as a work of the baroque era.

Something similar has happened in the interpretation of books of other great mystical and spiritual writers. For example, books expounding the most sublime kind of mystical theology, those of the great Doctors, St. John of the Cross and St. Teresa of Jesus, were accused before the Inquisition.

In regard to the censures and inquisitorial accusations, the *MCG* appears to be another chapter in the history of the accusations before the Inquisition against the books of the Mystical Doctor, with due allowance for differences in time. [10] For us, this effectively constitutes a counsel to examine the facts from a different and appropriate perspective so as to avoid the mistakes of the accusers. To insist on their accusations today is an injustice and a failure in objectivity, an insistence without any foundation in reality.

It is well known that during her lifetime Mother Agreda was indicted and accused before the Spanish Inquisition in much the same way as was St. Teresa of Jesus. On more than one occasion the examiners of the Tribunal of Logrono visited the Conceptionist Monastery in Agreda to subject her to rigorous questioning in view of an informative judgment, whose purpose was to determine the character of her spiritual

---

10 See my studies: E. LLAMAS, OCD, *Santa Teresa de Jesús y la Inquisición española*, Madrid 1972; and *Teresa de Jesús y Juan de la Cruz ante la Inquisición: denuncias, processos, sentencias...*, in *Cuadernos de Pensamiento* 7 (1993) 179-206.

comportment and the doctrine which she professed and imparted to her religious.

One of these visits was concluded by the examiner of the tribunal, Fray Antonio Gonzalez del Moral, a Trinitarian, on this occasion accompanied by the official Notary. At the end of their dialogue with the Venerable they confessed their "admiration" and recognized in her, as the official record records *"much virtue and great understanding of things pertaining to Sacred Scripture, acquired in prayer and continuous interior communion with God, rather than by study."* [11]

b) To put in perspective both the accusations against the *MCG* orchestrated outside Spain and in certain sectors of Spain itself from the 17th through the 19th century and the scant support given by the Church to her cause, one must remember that this work has been and still is today one of the most read of all Spanish literature, a fact amply demonstrated by its many editions and translations. [12]

The circulation which this work has won among those devoted to the Virgin Mary annuls the validity of the accusations. Simple folk who strive with love and without prejudice to approach the Immaculate Virgin via the *way of beauty* have discovered in this work the gospel image of Mary, that which the Church has offered us across the centuries, and have been able to relate spiritually to Her: to the Immaculate Virgin, the virginal Mother of the Son of God and collaborator with Him in the work of Redemption, the spiritual Mother of the Church and of each of the disciples

---

11 See J. Pérez Villanueva, *Historia de la Inquisición en España y América*, I (Madrid 1984) pp. 1072-1073. The officials of the Inquisition were so pleasantly surprised that they asked the Venerable Mother for icons and objects of devotion to take with them as souvenirs of the visit.

12 See: María de Jesús de Agreda, *Mística Ciudad de Dios, Vida de María*, text edited in conformity with the ordinal autograph, Introduction, notes by Celestino Solaguren, OFM, Madrid 1970 (reprinted 1982), pp. CII-CIV. All references are to this edition.

of Jesus, model and exceptional exemplar of holiness for all the faithful. This is the image which in summary fashion the text of Vatican II, and the recent Popes who have interpreted it, present us.

The image of Mary, writes Pope Paul VI with the teaching of the Council in mind, is the *tota pulchra*, is the *speculum sine macula* (the "all fair" and the "mirror without blemish"), is the supreme ideal of perfection, which artists of every age have attempted to reproduce in their works, is the "Woman clothed by the sun" (Apoc 12:1) in whom the purest rays of human loveliness meet the heavenly, yet accessible rays of supernatural beauty... Mary is the "fullness of grace" (Lk 1:28); or we might possibly say: she is the "fullness of the Holy Spirit, whose light is reflected in her with incomparable splendor... We must admire Mary, fix our glance on her unsullied fairness, because all too often our eyes are bewildered and as it were blinded by illusory images of human beauty." [13]

This is the precise, clear image of Mary which emerges from the pages of the *MCG*, and which illumines the texts of Mother Agreda. In such wise she admires the figure of Mary, fixing her eyes "on her unsullied loveliness," on her immaculate purity since her predestination. This is no mere simple phrase, or pious figure of speech. It signals the method and the procedure which she has followed in the composition of her work.

For this reason the *MCG* has been a source of satisfaction for so many simple souls who have actually read it and encountered in it, with enjoyment and spiritual profit, the authentic image of Mary: the gospel image and the living image of Mary offered us by the Church.

---

[13] PAUL VI, *op. cit.*, p. 338.

3. THE *MYSTICAL CITY OF GOD:* COMPENDIUM OF MARIOLOGY

a)   The *Mystical City of God* is a compendium of mariology. It is a perfectly structured work, not in a systematic form, as is the fashion with treatises of scholastic theology, but with a historical structure, that of the "history of salvation," the *Historia salutis,* arranged according to the chronological sequence of the mysteries in the life of the Mother of the Redeemer and of her Son. For this reason, this history is at the same time a theology, a mariology in our case, because Mary is the subject and content of reflection.

However, it is not a treatise of systematic mariology, along the lines generally followed by the commentators on St. Thomas and professional theologians, although there are a few exceptions. The mariology of the *MCG* is a *narrative mariology,* articulated about a number of historical facts and data. But at the same time these facts constitute theological data. For because of their special significance and on account of their supernatural teleology they are facts of salvation. Taken together they constitute a *historia salutis,* whose center is the mystery of the Incarnation of the Son of God, in which the Virgin Mary discharges an essential function. [14]

---

14 For this reason Mary forms an *essential part* in the mystery of our redemption. Pope Paul VI, in the document just cited, affirms precisely this, when he interprets the teaching of Vatican II in the light of a biblical text of St. Paul: Gal 4:4. Thus argues the Pope: *"The fact that 'in the fullness of time God sent his very Son, born of the Woman'* (Gal 4:4), *and that Mary as the Council teaches, 'was no mere passive instrument in the hands of God, but cooperated in the salvation of men with faith and freely given obedience'* (Lumen Gentium 56), *one deduces that Mary forms an essential part of the mystery of salvation."* Paul VI, *op. cit.,* p. 335. These statements of Paul VI represent a reaffirmation of the basic mariology of the *MCG.*

From this point of view the Venerable Mother Agreda, in the doctrinal richness which she brings to her work, in its breath and in the vivacity of its style, excels the mariologists of her day, viz., the commentators on St. Thomas Aquinas, and the authors of essays and studies on the Virgin.

One can speak appropriately of the *MCG* as a "compendium of mariology," because the authoress explains in its pages all the mysteries of the life of the Virgin Mary, the Mother of God, which at the same time are mysteries of her Son, the Redeemer. The explanation which Mother Agreda gives of these mysteries includes their theological and spiritual meaning. In relation to some of these fundamental truths one could hardly expect many details, for example, the eternal predestination of Mary, the realization of the Incarnation, the presence of Mary on Calvary, etc. Mariology is the explanation of the doctrinal content of these mysteries, which are mysteries of salvation, because Mary was so intimately united to her Son and was, by divine disposition, His Companion and collaborator in the work of salvation.

These descriptions of the mysteries of the Virgin Mary possess a theological content, and as such serve as concrete descriptions or representations of supernatural truths, in relation to and interacting with each other. This approach brings home to the reader and renders more understandable the reality and significance of the mystery.

This accounts, without doubt, for the attractiveness of this work to its readers. It is an aspect and value of the work which must be assessed with a certain detachment, keeping in mind that Mother Agreda wrote for an age when the baroque style was still a major force and enjoyed considerable influence on religious literature, and not yet subject to deformations and corruptions. The baroque influenced the conception and structure of her work, and left its mark on all its forms of expression.

From this point of view the value of the style is relative to the content, to the degree it corresponds to an objective appropriateness in expressing the content, or in the highest probable degree it finds some ground from within the normal unfolding of a biography. Historical and doctrinal errors pertain to and are situated in a category quite different from style. There is neither room for, nor presence of, such error in the pages of the *MCG*.

b)   Mother Agreda makes profuse use of imaginary figures and symbolic signs. These are devices, common to the style of her times, for achieving a certain plasticity in her explanations. Familiar as she was with the text of Sacred Scripture, it was only connatural for her to employ metaphor and images as symbols of supernatural realities. The very title of the work involves a symbolism, biblical in flavor: *Mary, Mystical City of God*, echoing authors from the patristic and medieval eras.

This symbolism affects the language and many expressions which aim at making accessible to us the ineffable: what is difficult to encapsulate in a single word. Thus, Mother Agreda indicates and assigns the dates of certain important events, so as to illustrate how they occurred in the middle of history. Hence, the birth of Mary is given as the eighth of September, and that of her Son the twenty-fifth of December, "at mid-night, on Sunday, and in the year of creation of the world as the Church of Rome teaches five thousand, one hundred ninety-nine." Mary when she became Mother of the Son of God was "aged fourteen years, six months and seventeen days." [15] These are liturgical reminiscences, which

---

15   *MCG*, Lib. I [*Lib.* is the abbreviated Spanish word for book], ch 21, n. 326, p. 146 [I, 263]; III, ch 10, n. 114, p. 389 [II, 45]; IV, ch 10, n. 475, p. 555 [II, 398].

on occasion are determined by symbolic exigencies, but in no wise are attempts to determine a precise historical moment from the point of view of chronology, at a distance of so many centuries...

4. THE MARIOLOGY OF THE *MYSTICAL CITY OF GOD* AND THAT OF VATICAN II

The history of the *Mystical City of God* has been darkened by censures and accusations surfacing within a very few years of its publication in 1670. These incidents disturbed the course of its history, but did not annul its beneficial influence upon a wide readership. Between 1670-1680 it was delated to the Spanish Inquisition, which at the highest level of appeal finally found it innocent of the charges and permitted its distribution and reading.

In 1696 five theologians deputed by the theological faculty of the University of Paris published a declaration wherein they harshly and rigorously condemned many propositions and affirmations of the *MCG* as contrary to the teaching of the Church. [16]

---

[16] I have referred here only to the two more significant instances as sufficient to make my point. For more information on these and similar cases cf. A. ARTOLA, *Dictamen Histórico-teológico sobre la Mística Ciudad de Dios*, in relation to the Cause of Beatification of the Ven. María de Jesús de Agreda, 1973, *passim* (unpublished typescript); A. ARTOLA, *La "Mística Ciudad de Dios" en la Sorbona. Un conflicto teológico a nivel europeo*, in *Universidad Internacional Alfonso VIII*: "El papel de Sor María de Jesús de Agreda en el Barroco español," Monografías Universitarias, no. 13, Soria 2002, pp. 195-208; IDEM, *La mariología, punto conflictivo en el proceso de canonización de la Ven. Madre Agreda*, in *Estudios Marianos* 69 (2003) pp. 21-41. E. LLAMAS, OCD-Agueda Rodríguez Cruz, *La 'Mística Ciudad de Dios' en el ambiente universitario y cultural de Salamanca en el sig. XVII*, in *Estudios Marianos* 69 (2003) pp. 273-301. I refer the reader to this volume 69 of *Estudios Marianos*: *La Madre Agreda y la mariología Española del siglo XVII*, Salamanca 2003, p. 430, which contains the acts of the study week at Soria (September 2-6, 2002) in honor of Mother Agreda. This volume

Today the Church, at the request of the competent authorities of the Diocese of Osma-Soria, has taken a renewed interest in these problems, with a view to reopening the prosecution of the cause of the Venerable Mother Agreda. At the conclusion of various transactions there was an official recognition of her upright and virtuous conduct throughout the various periods of her life, motivated always by a spirit of love for God and for the Church. Today there exists no doubt at all about her sanctity of life, confirmed by her spiritual writings, some still unpublished, and by the unanimous testimony of her contemporaries.

From the mariological and theological standpoint, the Sacred Congregation for the Doctrine of the Faith, on the basis of the report submitted by its Theological Study Commission, a report recommending study and analysis of the *Mystical City of God*, formulated its assessment as follows: "*One cannot assert that there exist in the* Mystical City of God *true doctrinal errors or heresies.*" Nonetheless, this notwithstanding, in the very same document a qualification is added to this assessment stating that *the presentation of the figure of the Mother of God found in this work* **contrasts with** *that which Sacred Scripture offers us, and* **is not compatible** *with the mariology developed by Vatican II.*

I was personally surprised by this restrictive conclusion; and I believe it will provoke the same surprise and will certainly be a cause of discomfort to all who are adequately acquainted with and read the *MCG* with a sense of objectivity and without prejudice. Why should the Commission want to affirm: "*it is not compatible*" with the mariology of Vatican II? Does this refer to the figure of Mary sketched by Mother Agreda, or to the mariology of the *MCG* in general?

---

contains twelve scholarly studies of great value on her life and on her work, the *Mystical City of God*.

At the very least it seems a bit disconcerting to state in a case like this that the *MCG* contains not a single doctrinal error and absolutely no heresy, that this assessment is certain, and in the very same breath claim that her mariology is not compatible with the mariology of Vatican II, which is the mariology of the Church.

The same point can be made in relation to the presentation of the figure of the Virgin Mary. If there are no doctrinal errors in the work of Mother Agreda, if it contains no heresy, how does it come about that the image which this work leaves us of the Mother of God does not correspond with the biblical and evangelical image offered us by the New Testament?… What image, then, is offered us, or how does it contrast with the one proposed and illustrated for us by Sacred Scripture?…

Of course, neither the image of Mary, which Mother Agreda offers us, nor her mariology would be found compatible with the mariology of Vatican II by anyone trying to interpret the *MCG* as a historical work in the narrow sense of that term, composed in a style and for a special purpose, according to the postulates of history and chronology. But the *MCG* is not this kind of work. Rather it is a work with a symbolic title: *Mystical City of God*. It is a *divine history*, as its very title makes clear, a spiritual history where history is a means of edification via examples, or a theological and spiritual interpretation of the mysteries of salvation, of the Virgin Mary and of the Redeemer, who made history among men, an excellent instance of the best hagiography of the baroque age.

Under the doctrinal aspect and from the point of view of what essentially constitutes the true image of Mary in a theological and spiritual sense, I find absolutely no incompatibility with the image of Mary which the Church offers us: the gospel image, which Pope Paul VI in *Marialis Cultus* defines and describes as "mirror" of holiness and virtue, just as Vatican II does, *who does not disappoint the profoundest expectations of men of our times.* [17]

In the face of these facts and considerations fully objective…how should one read and interpret this work? This is the problem. My intent is to recall here a number of basic "keys" to reading, of which not all readers have taken proper account, and thereby set in relief the fundamental coherence of the mariology of Mother Agreda with that of Vatican II, above all of its affinity and wonderful harmony with this Council on a number of points and specific themes.

---

17 PAUL VI, *Marialis Cultus*, 37; Cf. Vatican II, *Lumen Gentium* 65.

PART Two:

ELABORATION OF THE THEME

In this part I intend to describe the image of the Virgin Mary, the Mother of God as drawn by Mother Agreda, and make clear how in none of her fundamental features does this depiction of Mary **contrast** with the image offered us by Sacred Scripture. Quite the contrary: it will become quickly apparent from this exposition that this image of Mary is in full conformity with the biblical image of Mary, with that image as interpreted by Tradition and the living Magisterium of the Church.

Similarly, I intend to expound the fundamental mariology of the *MCG*, and its convergence and *full compatibility* with the mariology of Vatican II. For this, it is not necessary that a complete analysis be made of every page of the *MCG*. We may leave aside all that data and all those facts which this work provides with a view to filling in fittingly and harmoniously, all those gaps left in the life of Mary as this is recorded in the New Testament: dates and facts without biblical basis. Their discussion pertains to the literary genre of the work, but they are not to be considered wrong merely because not biblical. None of them, in fact, contains doctrinal errors or heresy. [18]

---

18 Nor should one consider the affirmation of such data an error. Such affirmation falls well within the limits of probability and possibility, and most of the time reflects a certain appropriateness. From this it does not follow that I am fully in agreement with all that the Venerable proposes on such points. Further, the greater part of this data pertains to the literary genre of the book. Fixing the number of Angels who guarded the Virgin Mary, or who accompanied her during the realization of some mysteries is a favorite flourish typical of the baroque.

1. THE BIBLICAL IMAGE OF MARY

In general, Mother Agreda does not claim as her specific goal a description or delineation of the image of Mary. Neither does she expressly identify her features or essential lines. But it is certain that the *MCG* contains very beautiful explanations, which may be considered as genuine descriptions of the image or portrait of Mary. [19]

a. General consideration

One should remember that Mother Agreda does not offer an exegesis, critical or scientific, of the texts of Scripture. This was not her objective. She interprets these according to their spiritual and theological sense within the limits and context of the history of salvation and of the spiritual life, in the style of the authors and spiritual masters of the 16th and 17th centuries. Her interpretations do not stand outside the context and scope of the texts themselves. Generally, she follows the interpretations made by other commentators, which were commonly accepted by spiritual writers of the time.

St. Teresa, for example, interprets a number of texts of the Canticle of Canticles, applying them to the Virgin Mary, in view of clarifying particular aspects of the highest mystical experiences, those she herself had experienced. [20] The Saint herself tells us that for about two years God had enabled her to *understand something of the particular meaning* enclosed

---

19 See for example *MCG* Lib I, ch 17, n. 252, p. 114 [I, 203 ff.]; and ch. 18, nos 268-269, 271, 282, pp. 122-123, 128 [I, 220-221; 230]; Lib III, ch 10, no 115, p. 389 [II, 95]: description of Mary at the Annunciation, at the moment of becoming Mother of the Son of God; and Lib IV, ch 10, nos 474. 475, p. 555 [II, 396-397]: Mary at the birth of her Son, etc.

20 See TERESA OF JESUS, *Meditaciones sobre los Cantares*, 6, 8 (in *Obras Completas*, Madrid 2000, p. 1076, 7).

in certain words, or *some understanding* of particular texts. [21] Could not the Venerable Mary of Jesus of Agreda have enjoyed a grace like that of St. Teresa? [22]

St. John of the Cross states in the Prologue of the *Spiritual Canticle* – offering a guide to reading it – that the abundance and dense content of texts of Sacred Scripture cannot be grasped as one would common terms in ordinary "use;" for this *they can never be explained verbally* except as the Holy Doctors **have spoken** and declared or **may speak** and declare. [23]

The words of Scripture, according to the Holy Doctor, enclose hidden mysteries, which God manifests to simple souls via the *via pulchritudinis*, the way of beauty, according to the terminology of Pope Paul VI, through contemplative prayer. Such prayer was a source of "wisdom" and knowledge of the Sacred Scriptures, which the Venerable Mary enjoyed, as her contemporaries were quite aware.

No one should be surprised, then, that she received enlightenment from God whereby she could discover the meaning of phrases of Sacred Scripture, and their relevance to the Virgin Mother of God and to specific events in the history of salvation, which other exegetes had missed entirely. However she accomplished it, the Venerable Mother managed to keep her interpretations of the Bible within the

---

21 "For some years the Lord has bestowed on me a great gift whenever I hear or read any words of the Canticles of Solomon... For about two years more or less the Lord has given me this gift to help me to understand something of the meaning of some words... Sometimes I understand so much that I desire not to forget, but do not dare to commit it to writing... But on hearing the opinion of persons whom I felt obliged to obey, I wrote down something of what the Lord had given me to understand..." St. Teresa of Jesus, *op. cit.*, 1041-42.

22 One might in this regard, and in the light of the texts of St. Teresa just cited in notes above, read this passage of the *MCG*: Lib. I, ch. 16, n. 243, p. 110 [I, 196-197]. Many other passages similar to this one can be found in this work.

23 St. John of the Cross, *Spiritual Canticle*, Prologue, no. 1.

bounds and with the character of Catholic exegesis and of the teachings of the most distinguished masters of the science of the spirit.

b. Some particular examples

If we turn our attention to particular instances, we can only be struck with wonder at the ease and mastery with which she interprets chapter 8 of the book of Proverbs as applied to the Virgin Mary, and chapter 12 of the Apocalypse, liturgical reminiscences of the era and biblical spirituality. A particularly important and especially valid idea is set forth in chapter 11 of the first book of the *MCG*, where taking the christological sense of creation and Mary's predestination as point of departure she tells us that "*in the creation of all things the Lord had before him Christ our Lord and His Most Holy Mother; and chose and smiled upon his people after the example of these mysteries,*" [24] so affirming the *association* of Mother with the Son from His predestination.

The sureness and theological precision with which the Venerable Authoress expresses herself is remarkable. She unravels concepts of our times and in dealing with a problem not highly elaborated in her era and which only today has met favor in the teaching of Vatican II, the "history of salvation," expounds it with the relevant terminology.

First, Mother Agreda has a very clear concept of the unity of the *historia salutis* in the eternal counsels of God. She is perfectly aware of the absolute primacy which Jesus Christ, the Son of God made man, occupies in this history, and of the singular role which the Virgin Mary, His Mother and Associate in the work of Redemption by divine disposition, discharges during the course of this history. Vatican II expressed this unity in terms of that bond linking the two

---

24 *MCG*, Lib. I, ch. 11, n. 134 ff., pp. 71-73 [I, 125 ff].

Testaments: Old as the preparation, and New, as the fullness of time and revelation of God. [25]

The fundamental idea of this chapter of the *MCG* includes the relation of the Mother with the Son, and her association in the history of salvation: two essential features of the authentic image of Mary. Mother Agreda from the very start of her exposition finds this mysterious association in Sacred Scripture, as is perfectly clear from her explanations beginning with Book I, chapter 5 of her work (pp. 37 ff. [I, 62 ff.]). And this is precisely the image of Mary which the Church has offered and continues to offer in the liturgy, in her ordinary Magisterium and in Vatican II.

In equivalent terms the Council affirms this fundamental feature of the image of Mary, namely, her association with her Son in the work of redemption, since His predestination and since the realization of the mystery of the Incarnation of the Son of God, when the Council states that Mary on becoming the Mother of God consecrated herself to the Person and work of her Son, serving with and under Him in view of the work of salvation. [26]

From this standpoint and on such premises, how can one claim that the image of the Virgin Mary offered by the *MCG* **contrasts** with that of Sacred Scripture? Mother Agreda has done nothing else but apply and develop the two fundamental principles, which are the backbone of mariology: the eternal predestination of Mary conjointly with the mystery of the Incarnation, and the soteriological worth and dimension of the Divine Maternity. She was predestined Mother of the Son of God, to be His collaborator in the Redemption. [27]

---

[25] Vatican II, *Dei Verbum*, 14-16.

[26] Vatican II, *Lumen Gentium*, 56, 61.

[27] This is a literal affirmation of Popes Pius XI and Pius XII. In these very terms the Spanish mariology of the 17th century was formulated. Cf. Pius XI, *Auspicatus profecto* (January 28, 1933) AAS

c. The biblical image of Mary

In the New Testament we encounter a descriptive *gospel image* of Mary, yet with well-defined features: an historical and spiritual image, sober and clear, of which Paul VI said that "it does not disappoint the deepest expectations of the men of our time." [28]

The same Pope set several features of this image in relief, thus correcting the explanations of certain minimizing authors, by pointing out its essential lines and describing the spiritual dispositions of the Mother of the Redeemer which make her the model for all the faithful. What is stated in the *MCG* relative to the image of the Virgin Mary is in conformity with the teaching of Pope Paul VI.

The historic image of Mary handed down to us by the Gospels is sober, and even if it is sketched only in its essential lines, this is sufficient to structure a *historical* and *narrative* theology of this mystery. The intention of Mother Agreda in her *MCG* was to fill in and adorn these limpid lines, and amplify the width and breath of that image with other moments and events of her existence. She sought to weave a history of that which in her opinion should have taken place in a normal and full development of the facts in the life of the Mother of God. This she did on the supposition that the Mother of God, qua protagonist of a singular history, such as the *historia salutis* – whose limits and whose content are defined and determined by the free will of God – is very much a singular person: the Immaculate, the Full of grace, the Virgin Mother of God. This "singularity," point of departure for many considerations, is expressly affirmed by

---

25 (1933) p. 80; Pius XII, *Ad coeli Reginam* (October 11, 1954) AAS 46 (1954) p. 634. These Popes allude to the biblical foundations of this doctrine.

28 Paul VI, *Marialis Cultus* (February 2, 1974), n. 37. [Hereafter abbreviated *MC*.]

Vatican II, when it says that Mary *was endowed with graces above every other creature, celestial and terrestrial*, and *for this reason is proclaimed super-eminent and absolutely unique member of the Church*.[29]

This singularity of Mary has its foundation in divine Revelation, as the liturgy and living Magisterium of the Church interpret it. Does all this **contrast** with the gospel image of Mary? At no point does this contradict the postulates of Revelation, which teaches us that Mary is truly the Mother of God, nor theology, which claims that the Mother of God enjoys a quasi-infinite dignity because of her relation with God, the infinite good to borrow the formula of St. Thomas Aquinas.[30]

In her work Mother Agreda has broadened the dimensions of the life of Mary, which from a historical point of view, seem to be excessively limited in the New Testament. In her pages she has included descriptions of other events. But as criterion for this she has faithfully taken account of what, within the context of the Gospel, would be the normal development of Mary's life, with special attention to her singularity and to the role which she discharged in the history of salvation. This history could very well have been the life and true image of Mary, of moments and events which the sources of Revelation guard over in silence. Nonetheless, the image which she offers us, in its fundamental lines, **is not in contrast** with Scripture.[31]

---

29 Vatican II, *Lumen Gentium*, 53.

30 ST. THOMAS, *Summa Theologica*, I, q. 25, a. 6, ad 6.

31 The Venerable Authoress of the *MCG* includes in its pages materials whose source is in apocryphal literature. All of these materials, however, are of secondary importance in the work as a whole, and within the context of the work as a whole and of its mariology play no significant role. On the other hand, the facts concerning the life of Mary found in apocryphal literature are not necessarily all wrong or false. Apocryphal is not a synonym of false. Facts apocryphal

For the rest, the gospel image of Mary, in so far as this has bearing on her interior dispositions and configures her personality, and as Pope Paul VI sketches it, [32] agrees perfectly in content with the descriptions and explanations which the Venerable Mother Agreda offers us in her work. The moment of the Annunciation, for example, when the Incarnation of the Son of God was effected, and the divine Maternity of Mary was realized, includes in the thought and description of Mother Agreda, Mary's spiritual dispositions of faith, love and obedience to the word of God. [33] This description is in full accord with the thought of Vatican II.

According to the Venerable Mother Agreda, Mary in speaking the words of acceptance of the will of the Father: ... *Be it done to me according to thy word*, initiated our redemption, with which she collaborated in a unique manner. [34] On its part, inspired by the text of St. Luke's Gospel, Vatican II asserts that the Virgin Mary became Mother of the Son of God in pronouncing those words: ... *Be it done to me according to thy word*, and consecrated herself from that very moment to the Person and work of her Son, serving with and under Him in the work of redemption. [35] She was *the beginning of our reconciliation* (Mother Agreda).

---

in origin and recorded by Mother Agreda are commonplace in the religious literature of her time.

32 PAUL VI, *MC*, 35.

33 See *MCG*, Lib. III, ch. 11, n. 138, p. 398 [II, 110]. Cf. my study: E. LLAMAS, La "Mística Ciudad di Dios," una mariología en clave de 'Historia de Salvación.' De la Madre Agreda al Concilio Vaticano II, in La Madre Agreda, una Mujer del siglo XXI: Universidad Internacional Alfonso VIII, Monografías Universitarias, no. 15. Soria 2000. P. 180-183.

34 *MCG*, loc. cit..

35 Vatican II, *Lumen Gentium*, 56.

d. In conclusion

In conclusion, the image which the Venerable Mother Agreda gives us of the Virgin Mary in her *Mystical City of God* does not **contrast** in its fundamental and essential features with the gospel image offered us by Sacred Scripture. She adds to it and broadens its dimensions, completes the facts and events of Mary's life, illustrates her features, singular lines and characteristics. But the Venerable authoress has not done this arbitrarily. Rather she has been guided by several principles, in conformity with the objectives and ends she proposes to realize in her work. All this, however, is kept within the limits of what one might reasonably suppose fitting, given the uniqueness of the person and of the mission of the Mother of the Son of God.

The adornments and complements with which the Venerable Mother has filled her *history* of the life of the All Holy Virgin do not contradict the gospel image, nor deform it. Quite the contrary: what she affirms of the Virgin Mary, from the doctrinal point of view, is based on principles which mariology has utilized since the onset of discussions of the Immaculate Conception in the middle ages and still utilizes: the principles of fittingness, of eminence and of singularity, which in its own way, Vatican II takes account of and accepts.

Acknowledging the eminent dignity of the Mother of God, and of her most singular mission in the "*history of salvation*," the great Masters have argued in the very same way on many occasions in view of their own objectives. For the Bible contains a history of salvation which is a message of life. The properly historical facts relative to the protagonists in this history and pertaining to the fundamental milestones of their existence have been kept to a minimum. It is perfectly licit, from a purely historical standpoint, to fill in the blanks so as to reflect the context of this history and other events consequent upon it, or to do the same thing from a spiritual and hagiographical viewpoint. Accordingly, the history, so narrated, seeks in part to amplify the message and explain the significance of the events recorded in the Gospel.

From a different approach one may ask: what positive value do lives and histories of Jesus Christ and of the All Holy Virgin possess? If we leave aside polemical questions concerning the Christ of faith and Jesus of history, and place ourselves within the perspective of the "history of salvation;" and if we read that history in the "kerygma" (proclamation of salvation) and the "kerygma" in the history[36] of the risen Christ, the Paschal Christ, it is neither strange nor absurd to reconstruct the life of Jesus Christ, or of the Virgin Mary. It is neither strange nor absurd to do this, introducing all those facts and events, which are the normal consequence of the daily comportment of the protagonists, taking account of the particular principles governing their lives. This is what the Venerable Mother Agreda accomplished in her great work: the *Mystical City of God*.

2. THE MARIOLOGY OF THE *MCG* AND THE MARIOLOGY OF VATICAN II

If the *MCG* does not contain true doctrinal errors, and nothing of what it teaches may be considered a "heresy," on what grounds can one claim that the image which it presents of the Virgin Mary is not compatible with the mariology developed by Vatican II? For exactly this claim is made in

---

36 B. FORTE, *La Cristología hoy: el desarrollo a partir del Vaticano II y las características emergentes*, in *Theologia Xaveriana* 142 (2002) p. 344.

the report of the Theological Commission of Study which examined this work in detail.

This claim rightly arouses surprise and shock in anyone who has closely examined the *MCG*. Does this surprise and shock arise because the claim is not objective, and does not correspond to reality? Or does surprise and shock arise because the Commission has redefined the concept of mariology so as to include in it dates and facts of history pertaining to chronological rather than historical study?

A possible **incompatibility** of the mariology of the *MCG* with that of Vatican II could have arisen from two main sources: from the structure or methodology of the work of the Venerable Mother, or from its doctrinal content (in relation to which history, as such, enjoys only secondary import). In view of such considerations, I believe that the *MCG* is fundamentally compatible with the Council document.

The analysis of this possible incompatibility entails two steps. Each pertains, or is in reference to some general aspect of the theme.

The first step is an examination of the doctrinal content of the *MCG* based on objective criteria, commenting on the actual texts of the Venerable authoress so as to arrive, on the basis of her own affirmations, at a conclusion concerning the compatibility of the *MCG* in its doctrine and in its formulation with the mariology of Vatican II.

The second step is an analysis of the "notes" distinctive of an authentic Catholic mariology, notes reflected in the teaching of the *MCG*. These notes: Trinitarian, Christological, Ecclesiological…are a guarantee of its full orthodoxy, and in the fundamentals of the *MCG* simultaneously manifest its harmony and coincidence with the mariology of the Council.

THE "MARIOLOGICAL CONTENT" OF THE *MCG* AND THE MARIOLOGY OF VATICAN II

A. MARGINAL DIFFERENCES AND SUBSTANTIAL UNIFORMITY

It is true that between the marian chapter of Vatican II, that *broad synthesis* – as Pope Paul VI describes it – of Catholic doctrine on the Virgin Mary, and the prolix text of the *MCG*, abounding in ideas and reflections on the Mother of the Son of God, there exist notable differences: differences in language, differences in the external structure of the text, in its length, in its references and authorities cited... Nonetheless, these differences pertain to factors touching the concrete composition of the text, its extension, its finality and objectives, and the diverse mind-set and other circumstances which accompany the origin of such documents. When, however, the two works are considered in relation to the soul and to the spirit which animates their content, one notes how these differences do not affect the formal and essential elements of mariology, whose character is properly doctrinal.

The Council offers us a micro-mariology, limited to principles, to fundamental affirmations, and to basic orientations. Given the finality of the text, there was no need to say more. Generally this text is sparing in its explanations, or arguments of a theological character. To the contrary the *MCG* is a macro-mariology, in which, sometimes excessively, prolix descriptions and explanations of the truths and fundamental dogmas relative to the All Holy Virgin abound, in a repetitive style, overloaded and exuberant in details, so characteristic of the baroque epoch. The text of the Council is linear, plain, and limpid in its embellishments and adornments, without parenthetical and accessory elements.

Yet, when one turns his attention to the essential lines and content of mariology, as it were to the features which configure the supernatural and authentic image of the Virgin Mary, there are found no radical differences between the *MCG* and the Mariological chapter of Vatican II. In view of this the statement that the mariology of the *MCG* is not compatible with that of the Council, sounds a discordant note.

The two texts present an identical image of Mary in her essential features: Immaculate, full of grace, predestined to be Mother of the Son of God conjointly with the mystery of the Incarnation, to be collaborator with Him in the redemption via the mysteries of His flesh, or of His life; Associate of the Redeemer in the mysteries of His Infancy, and above all, in those of His Passion; model of virtues, of faith, hope and charity, of obedience…, exemplar and type and Mother of the Church, gloriously Assumed into heaven, Queen of the universe; Mediatrix and Intercessor, recipient of that veneration due her in view of her excellence, superior to that of all creatures, angelic and terrestrial; all this relative to Christ, and via her maternity, related in a singular manner to the Persons of the Trinity.

Mother Agreda lingers long in expounding the presence and maternal role of Mary over the Church, principally after the death of Jesus until Pentecost, and thereafter, as

Mother and Teacher of the Apostles, so constituted there in an altogether special place of dignity by her Son. This is one of the most notable points of difference with the text of Vatican II. But as soon as a distinction between a juridical-sacerdotal order and one merely ministerial in the Church is introduced, there is nothing here incompatible with the mariology of Vatican II. In the final analysis, this maternal role was never anything more than a consequence and application of what Jesus himself said on Calvary: *Woman, Behold thy son* (cf. Jn 19:26-27), if one seeks to identify the content of this expression. The intuition here of Mother Agreda, spiritual and womanly, in no wise incompatible with the mariology of Vatican II, contributes details and important aspects of the maternal role of Mary in the first community of believers in Jesus.

B. STRUCTURE AND CHARACTERISTICS OF THE *MCG*

The *MCG* is a theological-spiritual history of the life of Mary, or a mariology with a historical-spiritual character, structured along the lines of the "history of salvation." The marian chapter of Vatican II may be described in precisely the same terms. It is a theological-spiritual vision of the life and of the maternal role of the Virgin Mary, organized according to the chronological order of her mysteries. In fact, this approach of the Council has been decisive for contemporary theology, opening on new perspectives, which have coalesced principally in a new vision and structure presently known as *historical christology*. Mother Agreda moved on this terrain, giving her mariology an orientation and a historical structure, without claiming in doing so, to be setting the example of a new style for conducting a theology of mind and heart.

On this precise fundamental fact the *MCG* coincides with the marian chapter of Vatican II. Msgr. G. Philips, redactor of the Council text, has set this historical dimension and structure of the chapter in relief. This dimension focuses admiration on the figure of Mary as *mystery – key word* in the Constitution on the Church. Thus, the first part of the chapter is equivalent *to a history of Revelation, from the first biblical pre-figuration of the Mother of the Messiah to her glorious Assumption.* Hence, his claim to have essayed a short *"biographical account of Mary, in so far as it is possible to realize a work of this kind taking the Scriptures as point of departure and in the light of tradition."* [37]

Following the guidelines of Sacred Scripture, interpreted in the light of the full revelation, the Council recognized the more important moments of the life of Mary, in which she collaborated with her Son in the redemption. Msgr. Philips made a synthesis of these facts of marian history, that which the Council text records. As a sequel he explained the homogenous unfolding of the truth, taking as his point of departure theological-spiritual reflection, *which does not discover new truths for us, but helps us to make transparent the ancient truths.* [38]

This kind of development, which in reference to the dogmas of the Immaculate Conception and Assumption, Msgr. G. Philips terms a *"subsequent evolution of dogma,"* [39] is precisely what Mother Agreda realized in her *MCG,* as fruit of a loving reflection, of meditative-contemplative prayer. In the same context Msgr. Philips calls this *"meditation in depth of which the Virgin of St. Luke provides us the example"* (l.c.).

---

37 G. Philips, *La Vierge au II Concile du Vatican, et l'avenir de la mariologie,* in *Maria. Etudes su le Sainte Vierge,* ed. H. du Manoir, tome VIII (Paris 1971), p. 48. See also pp. 54-58.

38 Philips, *op. cit.,* p. 58.

39 *Ibid.*

Here, it is important to note, Msgr. G. Philips seems to justify a far ampler treatment of the Virgin than that actually in the Council text where only a few examples and facets are found. This ampler treatment, which does not invent new truths, but merely clarifies the ancient marian truths, is exactly what the Venerable Mother accomplished in her work. The doctrinal content of that work may be classed as a development consequent upon general doctrine and reflection on the facts of history in the light of full revelation.

But still more important in this instance is the coincidence of methodology and structure in the work of the Venerable with the marian text of Vatican II, reaffirmed on the authority of Msgr. G. Philips, redactor of the text in question, and justified by his explanations, cited above.

Apart from doctrinal coincidences, the work of Mother Agreda presents other structural affinities with the Council text. The Venerable Mother follows the same procedure adopted by Vatican II, one developed synthetically. The two texts open with a consideration of the Virgin in the Old Testament. Next, the Council text underlines the Annunciation and mystery of the Incarnation, themes to which the *MCG* gives great importance. Both the *MCG* and the Council coincide in their understanding of these mysteries and the saving value assigned them... From here on the text of Vatican II mentions the more important moments of the life of Mary, which Mother Agreda explains in chronological succession.

I may be permitted to repeat here, by way of conclusion, by restating what I wrote in 1999 concerning the structure and doctrine of the *MCG: "The general teaching of Mother Agreda on the Virgin Mary relates perfectly and in precisely formal fashion with the thought and historical orientation which Vatican II has given to mariology."* [40]

C. "COINCIDENCES" BETWEEN THE *MCG* AND THE TEXT OF VATICAN II

There is copious data, objective and internal to the work of Mother Agreda, which demonstrates the statement concluding the preceding reflections. It is not possible to mention all of them. It will suffice to call attention to the more important from the point of view of the content of mariology.

1.   Mary in the Mystery of the Incarnation

a.   General consideration

The Incarnation of the Son of God is the decisive factor for mariology. It is the focal point of the very mystery of Mary, and the hinge on which all reflections on the All Holy Virgin turn. For in the fullness of time *God sent his Son, to be born of the Woman* (Gal 4:4). Mary, who was predestined from eternity to be the Mother of the Son of God, forms *an essential part* of this mystery. [41]

---

40 See E. LLAMAS, *La "Mística Ciudad de Dios," una mariología en clave..., op. cit.*, p. 173. This study contains other factual coincidences between the *MCG* and the Council text.

41 So Pope Paul VI declared in 1975, in a text meriting more attention than has been given it. Here is how the Pope interprets the doctrine of the Council: "From the fact that 'in the fullness of time God sent his Son to be born of the Woman' (Gal 4:4), and that Mary, as the Council teaches, 'was no mere passive instrument in the hands of God, but cooperated in the salvation of mankind in faith and free obedience' (*Lumen Gentium* 56), one realizes that Mary forms an essential part of the mystery of salvation." PAUL VI, *Allocution at the close of the International Mariological-Marian Congress*, Rome 1975 (AAS 64 [1975] p.336). When account is taken of this text which reflects the sense of the Magisterium of the Church interpreting the

The theology of the mystery of the Incarnation is the decisive factor in the configuration of the image of Mary and of the whole of mariology, which in content and structure must match those of christology. In this sense the image of the Virgin Mary presented by the Venerable Mother Agreda in her *MCG* possesses the same essential features as the image in the Council text. Mary's existence turns and entirely depends on the mystery of the Incarnation, and in view of this mystery, all other aspects of her life have been ordained. In virtue of this mystery Mary was from eternity predestined immaculate and preserved from all sin, full of grace and of the gifts of God. In view of this mystery Mary was clothed with the supreme dignity, *the highest prerogative and honor*, to use the wording of the Council, [42] to be Mother of the Son of God.

The mystery of the Incarnation, described with sublime simplicity in the account of the Annunciation, is the nucleus of the mariology of Vatican II, and the point of departure for further reflection. Msgr. G. Philips makes a special point of replying to those who have expressed surprise at the importance the Council text seems to ascribe to this mystery. [43]

---

mariological doctrine of Vatican II, many reflections and affirmations of Mother Agreda no longer seem exaggerations or oddities.

42 Vatican II, *Lumen Gentium*, 53.

43 He justifies its importance, and can refute charges of irrelevancy, because in ecclesial Tradition the Annunciation to Mary has been point of departure and basis for the entire development of marian doctrine, that is, of mariology. "Perhaps the importance given to the account of the Annunciation surprises more than one reader. The surprise will dissipate as soon as one realizes how in Tradition the Annunciation to Mary is point of departure and basis for all subsequent development of marian doctrine. It was in Nazareth, not on Calvary, where the ancient Doctors contemplated her who conceived the Savior in her heart before she conceived Him in her womb, in order to give light to the world." G. Philips, *op. cit.*, p. 56.

The mystery of the Incarnation in the *MCG* holds this same importance, acting as nucleus, root and basis of all that the Venerable Authoress expounds and comments.

The Council, in its introductory numbers, ponders the meaning of the mystery of salvation, bequeathed by the Son of God, and the singularity of the Virgin Mary, who received the Word of God in her soul and body, and gave light to the world. [44]

For Mother Agreda this mystery was the *sacrament of mercy*, revealing the great love of God for his creatures; [45] the greatest work and marvel of divine omnipotence; [46] the greatest work of divine power and of infinite wisdom; [47] the most excellent of the works of God *ad extra*. There exists nothing superior to or comparable with the Incarnation, and with the fact that God himself became man. [48]

b. *The consent of Mary*

So excellent a work necessitated a preparation on the part of the Virgin Mary, chosen to be Mother of the Savior. And it also necessitated – within the harmonious plan of salvation and the "condescension" of God – the consent of the Mother.

Vatican II states that the Lord was remotely and proximately preparing the Virgin Mary, *"adorning her with all those gifts befitting an office so great...enriched from the first moment of her conception with the splendor of a holiness altogether unique."* [49]

---

44 Vatican II, *Lumen Gentium*, 53.

45 *MCG*, Lib. III, n. 109, p. 387 [II, 92].

46 *MCG*, Lib. III, n. 123, p. 392 [II, 100]; n. 128, p. 394 [II, 103].

47 *MCG*, Lib. III, n. 135, p. 397 [II, 108]; n. 70, p. 374 [II, 68].

48 *MCG*, Lib. III, n. 136, p. 397 [II, 109].

49 Vatican II, *Lumen Gentium*, 56.

Mother Agreda extensively and profusely describes this spiritual preparation of the Woman fore-chosen and predestined to be Mother of God. And in this consists a coincidence of doctrinal content and orientation.[50]

In the times when Mother Agreda composed her work (1650-1665) only infrequently did mariologists dedicate a section or even a special paragraph to the *consent* of the Virgin in the Annunciation. Even Cristobal de Vega in his *Theologia Mariana*, one of the most complete works of his epoch, hardly refers to this topic.[51] Without doubt, on this point the Venerable Mother Agreda was in possession of an admirable and luminous intuition. She describes the circumstances of the young Mary and the cultural context in a manner similar to that of Vatican II, and with full precision and with phrases and expressions in full harmony with those of the Council explains Mary's acceptance of the message of the Angel.

---

50 See the chapters of Book II of the first part, and the first chapters of Book III of the second part.

51 C. DE VEGA, *Theologia Mariana, sive Certamina Litteraria de B. V. Genitrice Maria*, Naples 1866, 2 vols.

We may compare the two texts, taking account of the sobriety of the conciliar and the exuberant and baroque style of the Conceptionist Nun:

MOTHER AGREDA	VATICAN II
"… In his works *ad extra*…among which that of becoming man was greatest and most excellent, he did not wish to proceed without the cooperation of Mary Most Holy, and until she had given her consent. Thus, with and through Her he would bring to fulfillment all his works,… And so we would owe this great blessing to the Mother of Wisdom, our Reparatrix." *MCG*, Book III, ch. 11, n. 136, p. 397 [II, 109].	However, the Father of mercies willed that the Incarnation be preceded by the acceptance of the predestined Mother so that in this way, just as the woman contributed to death, so the Woman would contribute to life. Vatican II, *Lumen Gentium*, 56.
"…at the very hour of greatest Silence, she was called by the Lord Himself… The humble, prudent Queen replied: My heart is ready, Lord and Almighty King, for you to do with me as you please." *MCG*, Book III, n. 100, p. 384 [II, 85-86]	"The Virgin of Nazareth by order of God was greeted… She replied to the heavenly Messenger: *'Behold the handmaid of the Lord, be it done to me according to your word…'* *Ibid*.

Taking account of the importance and highest significance of the mystery of the Incarnation from the historical and salvific point of view, it is perfectly normal that the preparation of the Mother and of the events should unfold in a form and context similar to that described by Mother Agreda. Her thought coincides with the teaching of Vatican II, not only as regards the factual *consent* which Mary gave to the Messenger of God, but also as to the teleological dimension in that consent: the collaboration of the "woman" in the redemption. The Council contrasts her with Eve, recalling here a generally held thesis, and Mother Agreda calls her "Reparatrix."

The harmony of structure and content existing between the two texts is admirable. It is not my intention to adduce other, similar documentation. It suffices to take account of the fact that we are face to face with the great mystery of the Incarnation, which is "the work of the ages," as Pope Paul VI called it, citing St. Peter Chrysologus, [52] and which is the key to and point of departure of mariology.

Leaving aside, then, other facts and eloquent proofs of our thesis, and taking account of the fact that the mariology of the *MCG* is structured with the Incarnation as its point of departure, as is that of Vatican II, we believe that it is fully compatible with the conciliar mariology. This is confirmed by the coincidence of content and orientation existing in other themes fundamental and basic to Catholic mariology.

c.   *Collaboration of Mary in the Redemption*

In the preceding section we might have included other notable coincidences between the mariology of Mother Agreda and that of Vatican II. I refer to the meaning and soteriological value of the mystery of the Incarnation and of the consent: *consensus*, of Mary. This, however, forms part of a much more wide-ranging general question: that of Mary as collaborator with her Son in the work of redemption, which I desire to analyze and explain in greater detail.

1). CONCEPT OF DIVINE MATERNITY

The soteriological value of the *consensus* of Mary is a question typical of christological mariology and of the detailed soteriology expounded in contemporary mariology and in the marian chapter of Vatican II. Today it is commonplace

---

52 PAUL VI, *MC*, 37.

in theology to consider the Incarnation of the Son of God in the virginal womb of Mary in a soteriological sense, as the first saving act which the merciful Trinitarian love of God realized for the redemption of mankind. In this act the Virgin Mary cooperated efficaciously by her *consent:* with her faith, obedience and love, and so from her very own substance produced the nature assumed by the Person of the Word. This action was no mere biological function, because Mary was Mother of her divine Son "by the power of love," as the Venerable Mother Agreda says, and as contemporary mariology affirms. The divine Maternity was simultaneously a biological and spiritual action.

Here is what we find in the formulations or description which the Venerable Mother gives of this: "*The heart of the all pure Mary, by the power of a real and authentic love, gave and supplied the matter from which the most sacred humanity of the Word was made for our redemption.*"[53] Mother Agreda sets the divine Maternity, understood as biological and spiritual, in a soteriological context: the Word of God assumes the nature begotten for our redemption. What supplied *the matter was the heart, by the power of love,* because the Virgin Mary conceived her Son in her mind before conceiving Him in her womb, as St. Augustine affirms.[54] The Council, referring to the divine Maternity says this of Mary: *she received the Word of God in her soul and in her body;*[55] and elsewhere that "*believing and obeying, she begot on earth the very Son of the Father*"[56]. Faith and obedience are spiritual, supernatural actions. This coincides with what the Venerable Mother says in her *MCG*, when she states exactly that Mary supplied the matter from which was formed the body of Christ *by the*

---

53 *MCG*, Lib. III, n. 137, pp. 397.398 [II, 110].

54 St. Augustine, *Sermo* 215, 4: PL 38, 1074.

55 Vatican II, *Lumen Gentium*, 53.

56 Vatican II, *Lumen Gentium*, 63.

power of her charity and through her exercise of heroic virtues, [57] *exerting her faculties as far as these pertained to being a true Mother.* [58]

All this defines the environment of that sublime moment in which Mary spoke the words of consent: *Be it done to me according to thy word* (Lk 1:38), which made her Mother of God and associate in the redemptive work of her Son, cooperating with Him and under Him in the redemption, as Vatican II says. [59] Mother Agreda, then, describes this exceptional moment, in which Mary expressed her consent, and her obedience to the will of the Father, when she said: *Behold the Handmaid of the Lord, be it done to me according to thy word*; words *which were the beginning of our redemption.* [60]

Here Mother Agreda sets out an integral concept of the divine Maternity: a maternity at once biological and psychological-spiritual, in so far as the entire soul, full of divine grace is engaged. [61] The text of the Council in an identical context matches this, because today an integral concept of the divine Maternity is commonplace. The Council does not mention other features of this saving moment. Nonetheless, it expressly affirms that at this moment the Virgin Mary *consecrated her whole self to the Person and work of her Son,...so serving in the redemption.* [62]

2). ACTIVE COLLABORATION ALONG TRADITIONAL LINES

The collaboration of Mary in the redemption, as this is explained and taught by the *MCG*, is similar to and coincides

---

57 *MCG*, Lib. III, n. 147, p. 402 [II, 119].

58 *MCG*, Lib. III, n. 150, p. 404 [II, 122].

59 Vatican II, *Lumen Gentium*, 56.

60 *MCG*, Lib. III, n. 137, p. 398 [II, 110].

61 On this aspect of the essay see my study already cited: *La "Mística Ciudad de Dios," una mariología en clave...*, cit., pp. 180-183.

62 Vatican II, *Lumen Gentium*, 56.

with the conciliar mariology at many points. The marian chapter of Vatican II offers us a characteristic teaching on the active and objective – and I would also say *immediate* – collaboration of the Virgin Mary in the redemption of the human race within the context of discussions carried on by mariologists during the preceding decades. The declarations of the Council radically annul the minimalist theory of that group of theologians who defended a merely passive, receptive collaboration, restricted to the subjective order, and support the contrary theory, which professes an active and immediate collaboration in the objective redemption. [63]

The collaboration of Mary in the redemption is a core question for mariology. Hence on this point the teaching of the Council holds a special importance for us. For we are dealing with a question, after the divine Maternity the most important, and like the divine Maternity with a unique role in defining the specific structure and lines of mariology.

The approach of the Council to this theme ties in with the doctrine of objective, active collaboration professed by numerous theologians during the 17th century, in large part Spanish, who in fact form a school of thought on this theme. Mother Agreda is one of the most distinguished witnesses of this school in regard to this problem and in general of Spanish mariology during this century, the golden age of Spanish mariology.

It is easy to follow the unfolding of her thought, arranged according to the chronological order of the diverse moments or mysteries in the life of Mary, whereby she cooperated with her Son in the redemption of men. And it is also easy to pick

---

[63] On these theories which received major attention in mid-twentieth century cf. G. BARAÚNA, OFM, *De natura corredemptionis marianae in theologia hodierna (1921-1958)*. Romae 1960, pp. 94 ss. Also on this question one may usefully consult vol. XIX of *Estudios Marianos* (Madrid 1958).

out its coincidences with the teaching of the Council, because the Council follows an identical order and a like arrangement of these chronological moments, which also constitute the saving collaboration of the Mother of God, even if set forth in very summary form.

The coincidences of the *MCG* with the doctrine of Vatican II – or we might say with its mariology – are on this point very significant, and merit detailed consideration. For, on the one hand, we are dealing with a question which in the years immediately preceding the Council and during the Council was hotly debated. And, secondly, we are dealing with a classic theory, defended by the most authoritative mariologists of the 17th century, in accord with traditional theological teaching since St. Irenaeus.

3). A PRESUPPOSITION

The MCG *professes an active collaboration...* To clarify this entire problem, in the first place it must be recognized that the *MCG* contains a clear and precise teaching concerning the active collaboration of the Virgin Mary in the work of redemption: with her Son and subordinated to Him, which in its foundation and also in its form coincides fully with the teaching of Vatican II on this theme.

Mother Agreda, like the Council, teaches the intimate relation linking the divine Maternity and Mary's collaboration in the redemption. She also teaches, exactly as the Council does, although in abbreviated form, that Mary accomplished this saving collaboration by her love-charity, by her faith, by her obedience, by her sacrificial and spiritual oblation... Lastly, she teaches that the collaboration of Mary had universal character. Thus, from the form which this exposition takes she deduces how to analyze and interpret the fundamental moments of Virgin Mother's life.

On this the Council contains a concrete affirmation of supreme importance: "*The union of Mother and Son in the work of salvation was manifested from the moment of His virginal Conception to His death.*" [64] This collaboration is often set in relief and from the standpoint of human salvation takes on greater meaning in the more important moments of the Son and of the Mother, given the principle of association of Mother with the Son in the work of redemption, fundamental in the mariology of Mother Agreda.

In this regard the marian chapter of Vatican II has a text which fully recapitulates reflection on this problem. "*The All Holy Virgin…, by disposition of divine Providence, was on earth the exalted Mother of the divine Redeemer, above all other creatures His generous associate… Conceiving Christ, begetting Him, nursing Him, presenting Him to the Father in the temple, suffering with her Son as He died on the Cross, she cooperated in an absolutely unique way in the work of the Savior, with her obedience, faith, hope and ardent charity, with a view to the restoration of supernatural life to souls.*" [65]

I have transcribed this limpid text word for word, because it will serve as point of reference for our commentary on the *MCG*, which very clearly coincides with the thought of the Council. But it also enables us to know clearly and precisely the thought of the Council on the delicate problem of the collaboration of Mary in the work of salvation. It is not possible to call into doubt that the Council teaches and defends an active collaboration, exactly the contrary of the theory of passive-receptive collaboration, rejected also by the teaching of the *MCG*.

In another passage the Council cites and interprets a number of patristic texts, and concludes: "*With reason,*

---

64 Vatican II, *Lumen Gentium*, 57.

65 Vatican II, *Lumen Gentium*, 61.

then, the Holy Fathers believe that Mary was not a purely passive instrument in the hands of God, but cooperated in the salvation of men via her faith and freely given obedience." [66] And immediately after, a classic text of St. Irenaeus is cited: [Mary] *"by obeying became cause of salvation for herself and for the entire human race."* [67]

4). IMPORTANT MOMENTS OF COLLABORATION IN THE REDEMPTION

The Council not only affirms the fact of collaboration in the objective redemption, or "marian coredemption;" it also singles out a number of moments, or particular mysteries in the life of Jesus, in which His Mother collaborated with and under Him in the redemptive work. This is important. And it is in this chapter that we encounter the most striking coincidences between the text of the *MCG* and the teaching of Vatican II.

Mother Agreda in her *MCG* gives us an outline similar to that of the Council, much fuller, however, and far more articulated. She professes a genuine collaboration of Mary with her Son in the work of salvation during the more important and significant moments of His life. This chapter of her mariology is in full doctrinal harmony with the conciliar mariology, including a certain identity of terminology.

She understands the mystery of the Incarnation in a soteriological sense, as I pointed out above, and the divine Maternity in the integral sense, an activity which Vatican II, without detailing every aspect, summarizes in these words: *Conceiving her Son, begetting Him, "feeding Him," offering*

---

66 Vatican II, *Lumen Gentium*, 56.
67 ST. IRENAEUS, *Adversus Haereses*, III, 22, 4: PG 7, 959A.

Him to the Father... She cooperated in an altogether singular manner in the work of salvation... [68]

Mother Agreda moves in the same context. Moreover, she adds some important detail, as a spiritual assessment of her acceptance of the will of the Father.

In this regard the Council states that Mary, the Mother, consecrated herself to the Person and work of her Son..., assisting in the work of redemption. [69] The Venerable Mother understands this consecration as a sacrificial offering made to the Father, thus revealing the spirit of the word of God. Exactly as the Son of God on entering the world offered Himself to the Father: ...*here I am, O God, I come to do your will*, [70] so His Mother *offered herself as an acceptable sacrifice in His service, to nurse and "feed" her sweet Son, ready to assist and cooperate with Him in the work of redemption.* [71]

The Vatican Council, in the text cited, understands the *Presentation of the Child Jesus in the Temple*, as a true and proper saving action: *Presenting Him to the Father in the Temple...she collaborated in the work of salvation.* In regard to this mystery the Venerable Mother is very explicit, detailing most concretely the disposition of Mary:

> *She mirrored the work of the most sacred humanity of Christ, collaborating thus in the salvation of mankind. For His Majesty, who came down from heaven to be our Redeemer and Master, desired that His Most Holy Mother participate in a higher and most singular way the fruits of the general redemption...She collaborated in the work of salvation.* [72]

---

68 Vatican II, *Lumen Gentium*, 61.

69 Vatican II, *Lumen Gentium*, 56.

70 Hebr 10:6-7.

71 *MCG*, Lib. III, n. 151, p. 404 [II, 122-123].

72 *MCG*, Lib. IV, n. 579, p. 604 [II, 490-491].

Finally, the Council teaches that the Virgin Mary, at all these moments, and in the last ones of His life, collaborated in the redemption via her spiritual disposition, by her faith, her charity, her obedience...[73] This is exactly what Mother Agreda says more than once: collaboration by faith and obedience,[74] by an ardent charity.[75] Her teaching also coincides with that of the Council when she says that Mary's faith influenced the mystery of the Incarnation, which was the beginning of our redemption, as we have seen elsewhere.

There is no need to accumulate texts from the *MCG* to illustrate its coincidence and compatibility with the mariology of Vatican II. It suffices to take account of the following text which is relevant to both themes, and this in perfect conformity, even in terminology and in certain phraseology, with the living Magisterium of the Church, from Pope Leo XIII to our days. Mother Agreda writes thus:

> *Wondering at this exaltation of Mary Most Pure and at how she was Mediatrix and portal for all the predestined, I was given to understand that this prerogative befits her office as the Mother of Christ, and what as Mother she did for men conjointly with her Most Holy Son. For she furnished Him from her own very blood and substance a body, in which He suffered and redeemed men. Thus on account of her unity with His flesh and blood, She in a manner died and suffered in Christ; and more than this she accompanied Him in His passion and death, and willingly suffered with Him according to her power with divine humility and courage. And as she cooperated in His passion and offered herself with her Son as victim for the human*

---

73 Cf. Vatican II, *Lumen Gentium*, 61; see also nos. 56 and 63.

74 *MCG*, Lib. IV, n. 519, p. 576 [II, 488].

75 *MCG*, Lib. I, n. 299, p. 134 [I, 242].

race, so also the Lord himself made her participant in His dignity of Redeemer, and placed her in charge of the merits and fruits of the Redemption... [76]

2. Further Coincidences

The teaching of Mother Agreda on the collaboration of Mary in the work of redemption also coincides with that of Vatican II on other points. I detail here only a few of the more important, which have doctrinal significance, as well as an ecumenical dimension and application.

a. By divine dispensation

By this I mean to set in relief how in the *MCG* the Venerable Mother affirms more than once, that the Virgin Mary collaborates in the redemption, not by reason of her being or nature, nor in virtue of the exigencies of a natural or supernatural context, but rather in virtue of divine disposition, as Vatican II reminds us: *by the grace of the omnipotent God.* [77]

To be Coredemptrix was for the All Holy Virgin a grace and a gift, which Jesus Christ himself wished to grant and in fact granted to His Mother, as we have seen in the text just cited above, and can be seen in other parallel texts. [78]

b. The Difference between the action of Jesus and the collaboration of Mary

Lastly, Mother Agreda distinguishes with precision between the redemptive action of Jesus Christ and the "act of collaboration" of His Mother. This latter in no way can be

---

[76] *MCG*, Lib. I, n. 275, p. 125 [I, 224-225].

[77] Vatican II, *Lumen Gentium*, 56.

[78] Cf. *MCG*, Lib. IV, n. 579, and *passim*, p. 604 [II, 490-491].

the equivalent, neither in its value nor in its efficacy, of the action of the Son. Jesus Christ is the Redeemer and Mediator absolutely. The collaboration of Mary is a proportional participation. Even if on occasion the Venerable Mother seems to speak of equality, something she never affirms in the strict sense, in fact on these occasions she has in mind an equivalent proportion, or proportionality, that is, relatively. Such relativity entails a kind of equivalence, because one deals here with a single action bearing on a single object: the redemption of mankind; but also entails inequality in view of a certain proportionality between Son and Mother, because of the intrinsic value and efficacy of this single work: absolute in Jesus Christ, relative in the Virgin Mary. [79]

Mother Agreda, however much she exalts the value and singularity of Mary's collaboration in the redemption, equally affirms its difference and inequality in relation to the action of the Redeemer, intrinsically of infinite value, because it is the saving action of the Word of God. In general this is what

---

[79] Important in this regard is the text of chapter 18, Book I, where she affirms that all the Virgin Mary has received has been granted her by God, or her Son, in a measure determined by her relation to Him. In the supernatural order *"the measure (of all things) is Christ Himself,"* and in Her a measure *"appearing equal and proportionate to the high dignity of the Mother"* No true or absolute equality between two measures is affirmed here; "the relative proportion appears..." *"in the length of her gifts and blessings, and in the breath of her merits, in all she was equal (proportioned to Him) without defect or disproportion (inequality). By no means could she absolutely equal her all holy Son, in terms of that equality which the professors call mathematical, because the Christ, Our Lord, was both man and true God whereas she but pure creature; and for this reason the measure of Christ infinitely surpassed that which was measured by it. Nonetheless, Mary Most Pure enjoyed a certain proportionate (or comparable) equality (measure) with her most holy Son... Nothing was lacking to her nor could anything appropriate to her or due her as true Mother of God himself be lacking in perfection. Thus to Mary as Mother and to Christ as Son were conceded like (equal) proportions of dignity, of graces and gifts, and of merits; and no created grace was in Christ which was not found proportionately in His Most Pure Mother."* MCG, Lib. I, n. 278, p. 126 [I, 227]; see also Lib. V, n. 955, p. 794 [III, n. 15, p. 15 ff.].

Vatican II says with a different terminology. The collaboration of Mary is by divine disposition. The redemptive work of Jesus is His in virtue of His very nature and condition, is properly His. [80]

c. Conclusion

From all these testimonials which I have adduced and commented on here – and they are only a sample – we may deduce one clear, precise conclusion: the image of the Virgin Mary which the Venerable Mother Agreda offers us in her *MCG*, and indeed its mariology, coincides in basics with that of Vatican II, and for this very reason is compatible with the mariology of that Council. [81]

I leave aside any further examination here of other texts illustrating how the mariology of Mother Agreda matches that of Vatican II, and in particular other moments of the life of the Virgin Mary and of her collaboration in the Passion of her Son. Those desirous of a more extensive exposition of texts bearing on this theme may find such in other works, [82]

---

80 Vatican II, *Lumen Gentium*, 60-62.

81 This conclusion is not a novelty. I have explained and defended it in other studies, which the reader may consult. These are: *La "Mística Ciudad de Dios," una mariología en clave de historia de salvación. De la Madre Agreda al Concilio Vaticano II*, in *La Madre Agreda, una Mujer del siglo XXI:* Universidad Internacional Alfonso VIII, Monografías Universitarias, n. 15. Soria 2000, pp. 172-178; *La cooperatión de María a la redención en el siglo XVII y en la Madre Agreda (Mistica Ciudad de Dios)*, in *El papel de Sor María de Jesús de Agreda en el Barroco español:* Universidad Internacional Alfonso VIII, Monografías Universitarias, n. 13. Soria 2002, pp. 209-238; *La colaboración de María a la redención en la "Mística Ciudad de Dios" y en la mariología española del siglo XVII*, in *Estudios Marianos* 69, Salamanca 2003, pp. 131-155; *The Immaculate Conception and Marian Coredemption in the* Mystical City of God *of the Ven. Mary of Agreda*, in *Mary at the Foot of the Cross V,* New Bedford MA 2005, pp. 393-440.

82 See note 81.

where I have set in relief the compatibility of Mother Agreda's mariology with the marian doctrine of the Council.

3. Two Important Moments: Mary at the Ascension of the Lord and at Pentecost

a. *Filling gaps in, or breaking the silence of the New Testament account of Mary*

Mother Agreda teaches that the Risen Christ appeared first to His blessed Mother. She had been readied and prepared for this with diverse favors bestowed on her by her Son. As to the truth of this appearance, the Venerable Mother's view agrees with an interior locution of St. Teresa of Jesus, and with the opinion of other authors. [83] What had Mary to do after the Resurrection of her Son? The redemption had been completed. Jesus had instructed His Apostles during paschal tide on the evangelization and the proclamation of the message of the Gospel to all nations. What is the significance of the presence of Mary for the primitive Christian communities, that of Jerusalem, of Capernaum, perhaps of Bethany, of Samaria? What is the meaning of her presence at Pentecost?...

1) Jesus from the Cross had proclaimed Mary Mother of the Church, a Mother for His disciples, represented in John: *Woman, behold thy son...* After which He said to the disciple: *Behold thy Mother* (cf. Jn 19:26-27). The son took her into

---

[83] MCG, VI, ch. 26, n. 1471, p. 1074 [III, n. 760, 732]. As regards the present state of the question *re* the views of St. Teresa of Jesus concerning this first appearance of the Risen Savior to His Mother, cf. the explanatory note for passage n. 13, 12 of St. Teresa's *Cuenta de Conciencia*, in TERESA DE JESÚS, *Obras Completas*, Madrid 2000, pp. 989-990. This theme has recently been discussed by theologians, with considerable animation, because of a remark of POPE JOHN PAUL II about this first apparition of Jesus: "*It is legitimate to believe as true that Mary was the first person to whom Jesus appeared after His Resurrection.*" (*L'Osservatore Romano*, May 22, 1997, p. 4.)

his home. All the Apostles recognized her as such, and as such venerated her. Among the disciples Mary's comportment was such as befitted the Mother of their Master and Head. What did she do with these disciples during paschal tide?...

The sacred books maintain a respectful silence on the figure and activity of the Mother in those first Christian communities. Nonetheless, with that silence they suggest more than they say. "Acts," after citing the names of the Twelve simply says they *continued with one mind in prayer with the women and Mary, the Mother of Jesus, and with His brethren* (Acts 1:12-14). Acts describes a few activities of the Apostles and events of the first communities. But in general it remains silent concerning Mary.

This could well seem surprising, given the dignity bestowed on the Virgin Mary, and the role she had played with her Son in the redemption of the human race. Mother Agreda, however, via supernatural channels, has found a solution for this silence. She understood the following in prayer, as a manifestation and "reply" of the All Holy Virgin herself:

> *And because you are once again in wonder that the gospels do not describe the works of the Savior done with me, I will explain to you... I myself ordered the Evangelists not to write anything about my many privileges beyond what was necessary to establish the Church on the articles of faith and commandments of the divine law.* [84]

Mother Agreda in the *MCG* intended to complete the account of Acts, with dates, activities and events, those seemingly most normal and fitting, within a spiritual order

---

84 *MCG*, VI, ch. 28, n. 1508, p. 1094 [III, n. 797, 769]. The Venerable Mother transcribes these words of the Virgin as a reply, as though she had previously asked a question, which in this case perhaps is the equivalent of a vivid and strong desire to know...

and a singular environment, in which the Mother of Jesus as protagonist had taken a personal and special role. Proclaimed by her Son spiritual Mother of the Church she did not thereby lose her dignity as Mother of God and as Associate and Collaborator with her Son in the redemption. And this fact deserved and postulated respect in the primitive Church and a very special consideration.

2) A number of medieval writers, theologians and historians during the first half of the 17th century employed an identical format for their writings. The revelations of St. Brigit, so widely circulated in every age, aim at completing the history of the mysteries of the Infancy and Passion of Jesus Christ. Authors of the 14th and 15th centuries have written edifying pages of exquisite beauty with the same objective: to break the silence of the New Testament on the history of the Son of God in relation to the more important steps in His life: Incarnation-infancy, passion-resurrection… Ubertino of Casale (+ c. 1325), to cite but one example, offers us in his *Arbor Vitae* intuitions and suggestions in no wise strange or implausible, either in relation to the events in themselves or in relation to their interpretation. [85]

The exposition of Ubertino of Casale possesses considerable affinity with the texts of Mother Agreda. He, too, adopts a dialogue style, inventing conversations between Mother and Son, but more sober and less elaborate that those of the Venerable Mother. The scenes unfold in both cases within an identical context, with an identical rhythm, and in the same spirit. Referring to the mission of Mary after the Resurrection of her Son, Ubertino mentions how the Virgin implored Jesus that on completion of the redemption of the human race, He take her with Him to heaven. Jesus,

---

85 On Ubertino of Casale, author of the *Arbor Vitae*, see L. GAMBERO, *Maria nel pensiero dei teologi latini medievali*, Naples 2000, pp. 325-338.

consoling her, replied with the tenderness of a son that this would be very hard on the Apostles and on the first disciples, for they would be deprived at once of the presence of the Mother and of the Redeemer Son. [86]

Later, mariologists and historians, contemporaries of Mother Agreda, wrote works similar in structure to the *MCG*, although more sober and less long-winded, in which they contemplate and describe the figure of Mary with identical features, and give her the title of Teacher of the Apostles. José de Jesús María Quiroga does just this during the very years when the Venerable Mother was composing her work (1652-1656). In reference to the days immediately after the Resurrection of Jesús Quiroga states that in those days the blessed Mother began *indeed to enjoy the office of Teacher of the Apostles, for which God left her behind in the Church*[87].

In a way it is legitimate to ask: how was the situation in which the Mother of Jesus lived in relation to the Apostles and the primitive Church structured? What did the prerogative of being the spiritual Mother of the Church imply and what did it include? The wide-ranging explanation of Mother Agreda is consistent in its basics with what had already been affirmed by medieval authors, and what was taught in the mariology of her day, and what has become common doctrine in the Ecclesiastical Magisterium of our time. On this

---

86 "*The kindest of Sons replied in a very respectful and consoling tone... It would be much too hard on them to be deprived simultaneously of me, shepherd and father, and of you, mother and teacher.*" UBERTINO OF CASALE, *Arbor Vitae*, Lib. IV, c. 29, f. 175. The coincidences between this author and Mother Agreda are not only in the realm of concepts and ideas; they are also structural and appear in the delineation and description of different levels in the life of the Virgin Mary.

87 JOSÉ DE JESÚS MARÍA QUIROGA, *Historia de la Vida y Excelencias de la Santíssima Virgen María, nuestra Senora*, Madrid 1957, Lib. V, ch. 1, p. 1117. This work first saw the light in Amberes in 1652, and enjoyed a second edition with wide circulation, Madrid, 1656-1657.

presupposition can one plausibly claim that her mariology is incompatible with that of Vatican II?

b. Mary, Mother and Teacher

In the situation faced by the Church during her first years, in that slow and steady work of evangelical expansion, of clarification and strengthening of the faith and of placing charity on a firm footing, Jesus constituted His Mother as Mother and Teacher of the Church, as Mother and Queen.

In effect, she who was spiritual Mother of the Church, proclaimed as such by Jesus Christ from the Cross on Good Friday, had to carry out this spiritual ministry. Her presence in the Church, as Pope John Paul II teaches, is a maternal presence and mediation. [88] Within this role is included whatever properly pertains to maternal guidance and instruction, specifically in relation to the disciples of her Son.

With the Resurrection of Jesus the redemption was complete, and for the same reason Mary's activity as Coredemptrix had ceased. Here she began that other mission in relation to the Church which the entire Blessed Trinity had entrusted to her: that of *Mother and Teacher*. The Venerable Mother simply assumes this as established fact: namely, the official inauguration of the mission of Mary in the new Church, and then proceeds to explain her various roles:

> *Of this blessing and of those I will mention further on,....Mary Most Holy has shown herself to be of a lineage sharing the dignity of her Son, the terminology to explain which I lack; for it gives her a communication in His attributes and perfections corresponding to the ministry of 'Mother and Teacher of the Church,' in the*

---

88 JOHN PAUL II, Encyclical *Redemptoris Mater*, 25 March, 1987, nos. 38 ff.

*place of Christ Himself, and elevates her to another, new
level of knowledge and power.* [89]

We know little of this magisterial mission of Mary, and
of the place which she occupied in the Church. She was not
invested with sacerdotal dignity; she did not emerge in public
as missionary or preach the message of the Gospel in the cities
and to the people of Israel. Jesus Christ appointed St. Peter
as Prince of the Apostles and His Vicar on earth. But on His
Mother he bestowed a *new level of being in knowledge and
power*, without qualifications of any kind. For this reason,
without doubt, she occupied a singular place in the Apostolic
College and in the primitive Church, as *spiritual Mother* and
as *Teacher*.

The thesis of Mother Agreda on this point is well defined,
and does not require further clarifications. Systematic
mariology has hardly felt the echo of this idea, for the rest
so befitting the dignity of the Mother of the Redeemer, and
so in accord with the meaning and content of her spiritual
maternity, proclaimed by her Son on Calvary: *Woman, Behold
thy son* (Jn 19:26). Narrative and hagiographical mariology,
that of the *MCG*, and kerygmatic mariology, of which the
17th century boasts many, authoritative masters, has paid it
great attention.

Besides all this the recognition of this prerogative *Mary,
Teacher of the Apostles*, is proven by other reasons and by
much other documentation. Iconography, too, provides
instructive witness along this line. As an example an icon
of the Ascension of the Lord will serve. It reproduces a

---

89 *MCG*, Lib. VII, ch. 28, n. 1501, p. 1091 [III, n. 790, 761 ff., here
763]. Mother Agreda, accustomed to situate more important and
surprising events by recreating their scene in plastic form, and then
describing it in baroque style, imagines here a vision of the Virgin
Mary in which the three divine Persons, each in a manner proper to
himself, entrust her with the mission of *Mother and Teacher* in favor
of the Church.

scene typical of the ancient Byzantine iconography which represents the glorious Christ as *Pantocrator*, rising to heaven between two Angels and blue circles. Beneath Christ is seen the Virgin Mary kneeling, in a position of prayer, as Mother, Teacher and exemplar of the Church, represented in the group of Apostles and of other disciples at either side of her, in veneration and all attentive. All are in admiration, except her, a gesture thus insinuating that in the absence of Christ who is leaving earth, She will be His representative, His presence, Mother and Teacher of the Church. [90]

c. Spiritual maternity and magisterium of Mary

Face to face with the abundance of "secondary themes" which might be considered in this context, I want to stress the importance of that theme which Mother Agreda perceived during her contemplative prayer concerning the life of Mary: *Mary, Mother and Teacher.* In her times such questions were novelties. Few mariologists made reference to them, or only analyzed them from a historical and doctrinal standpoint.

It was not common in her time to use these titles: *Mother and Teacher*, of the Mother of Jesus and assign her such roles in the Church. Mother Agreda, as a contemplative soul, found in them a happy "intuition," fruit without doubt of the sapiential knowledge with which she was endowed, and which she had attained in prayer. Systematic theologians, commentators on St. Thomas around the middle of the 17th century, lacking this wisdom and strangers to this concern, ignored the problem, or paid it scant attention.

---

[90] The icon venerated in the Sanctuary of Our Lady of Loreto in Ulldemolins, Tarragona. Two angels clothed in white are behind the Virgin, and are speaking to the Apostles, informing them of the mission of the Mother of Jesus in His absence. She remains with them as Mother and Teacher of the Church.

It is, on the other hand, certainly significant that spiritual mariology, represented by authors specializing in a kind of applied mariology (Pedro de Bivero and Cristóbal de Vega), in particular authors who systematized mystical-scholastic theology (17th and 18th centuries), for example Joseph of the Holy Spirit, decidedly affirms this prerogative granted by Jesus to His Mother: *Teacher of the Apostles*. Authors of this kind explain that prerogative and adduce valid proofs and arguments from authority in its favor.[91]

1). THE THEME IN MOTHER AGREDA

In addition to what we have hitherto affirmed and explained, close attention must be paid to the fact that Mother Agreda dedicates entire chapters (the last of Book VI and the first of Book VII) to fill gaps in the account of the life of the Mother of Jesus left us in the *Acts of the Apostles*. As ground for this effort it would seem absolutely reasonable that *Acts* should record some basic data on her maternal presence in the primitive Christian community, if the title of Mother of the Church, proclaimed by her Son on Calvary, connotes important content, as in fact, is the case. For this reason the approach of the Venerable Mother is fully justified within the context of a proposed history of the life of Our Lady. All that she says is appropriate, even if at times the descriptions of the events are bombastic and excessively prolix. But all of what is so described, or could have happened in similar form, either in corporal form or in that of a spiritual-intellectual

---

91 It is important to keep in mind that this theme, foreign to systematic-speculative mariology in Mother's time, is common and familiar in the *theology of mind and heart*. The Carmelite, Joseph of the Holy Spirit (1667-1736), who systematized mystical-scholastic theology, ascribes this same title to Mary: *Mary, Teacher of the Apostles*, explains it and adduces theological proofs for it. Cf. JOSEPH OF THE HOLY SPIRIT (from Andalusia), *Cursus Theologiae Mystico-scholasticae*, ed. P. Anastasius of St. Paul), vol. IV (Bruges, Belgium, 1931), disp. XXII, nos. 25-25.

or imaginative vision, and so remains within the realm of possibility.

In these chapters she frequently gives the Mother of Jesus the titles of Mother and Teacher, who with her maternal assistance and instruction helps to plant the new Church in the world.[92] At times she gives these titles to Mary, alluding to her activity and to her presence in the apostolic Community. Occasionally she gives Mary the title of *"Teacher of humility."*[93]

The *magisterium* which the Mother of Jesus enjoyed was not an ecclesial institution, but a personal prerogative, consistent with her dignity as Mother of the Son of God, with her collaboration with Him in the redemption, and with her role as spiritual Mother of the disciples of Jesus.[94]

These considerations of Mary, "Mother and Teacher of the Church," "Mother of the Apostles," may perhaps cause surprise in some readers and scholars. As the title itself, so above all the frequent extraordinary phenomena with which the Authoress accompanies the life of the Virgin during paschal tide before Pentecost, set in relief the Virgin's communication and association with her Risen Son. These are the embellishments of her hagiographical style. The Venerable Mother wrote about these mysteries of the life of Jesus as periods of contemplative prayer drew to a close. Such

---

92 So states the title of ch. 1, Book VII, p. 1123: How she has been lifted up to heaven to share in the glory of her Son in the Ascension and remains on earth *that the Church might be planted with her assistance and magisterium.*

93 JOSEPH OF THE HOLY SPIRIT (from Andalusia), *Cursus Theologiae Mystico-scholasticae*, ed. P. Anastasius of St. Paul), vol. IV (Bruges, Belgium, 1931), disp. XXII, nos. 25-25.

94 On "Mary Mother and Teacher" in Mother Agreda, see: G. CALVO MORALEJO, *María, primera discípula de Cristo, Madre y Maestra de la Iglesia, en la Madre Agreda*, in *La Madre Agreda, na Mujer del siglo XXI*: Universidad internacional Alfonso VIII, cit., pp. 243-261; IDEM, *María Madre de la Iglesia y Maestra de los Apóstoles en la Madre Agreda*, in *Estudios Marianos* LXIX (2003) pp. 157-180.

comportment of the Son with His Mother appeared to her perfectly normal for persons who belong more to heaven than to earth, especially after the Ascension of the Lord.

However, neither surprise over, nor odd vibes on meeting the theme of Mary's *magisterium,* can be cause or sufficient motive for claiming that the marian doctrine of the *MCG is not compatible* with the mariology of Vatican II. The fundamental idea in this part of the work (Books VI-VII) is that after the Ascension of the Lord to heaven Mary exercised a special role as Mother and Teacher of the Church, by word and example. Her presence reached a high point on the day of Pentecost, when in the Cenacle She was united with the Apostles and the pious women in prayer, as true Mother and Teacher of the first Christian Community.

2). MARY, TEACHER OF THE APOSTLES AND THE PRESENT MAGISTERIUM OF THE CHURCH

This idea, a fundamental teaching of the *MCG*, ignored by systematic mariologists until very end of the 19th century, has become commonplace in post-conciliar mariology. Since the years of Pope Leo XIII, and thanks above all to the spirit and doctrine of some of his Encyclicals on the Rosary, it has recently become a theme present in the mariology and official teaching of the living Magisterium of the Church.

This thesis has become familiar in post-conciliar mariology, which considers the *magisterium* of Mary as an exercise of her maternal role and an expression of her maternal presence in the Church. Mary is a type of the Church, is her exemplar, Mother and Teacher of the disciples of her Son, who educates them in the faith and in the ways of spiritual life. [95]

---

95 An author who has painstakingly studied this theme in our days is His Eminence CARDINAL ANTONO MA. JAVIERRE. See his study: *Maria, Madre y Maestra*, in *Ephemerides Mariologicae* 30 (1980) 85-105;

The teaching and the activity of the Magisterium of the Church in regard to this theme is a guarantee of its truth. At the same time it is a clear manifestation of the internal power of the teaching of the word of God, and in our case of the proclamation of Mary on Calvary, as *Spiritual Mother of the Church: "Mother Behold thy son,"* and of the homogeneous unfolding of this truth under the action of the Holy Spirit in a double direction: as a deepening of the truth itself and as an extensive application in accord with the signs of the times.

The express teaching of the Church on this point begins with Pope Leo XIII. It is important to reflect on this data, because thereby we will discover how it corresponds with the mariological teachings of Mother Agreda. At the same time such reflection helps to disclose still another proof that the mariology of the *MCG* is doctrinally compatible with that of Vatican II.

Pope Leo XIII firmly teaches that the Virgin Mary fulfilled a magisterial role in relation to the Apostles and to the primitive Church after the death of her Son. It is useful here to recall the personality of this great Pontiff, who introduced the Christian Church to the 20th century, who codified principles and new ideas for the renewal of society and of the Church. These were among the factors defining his life and apostolic mission.

In regard to mariology and marian piety of the Church great importance is held by the formulation of the mission which the Mother of the Redeemer enjoyed during the

---

IDEM, *María, Madre y Maestra. Meditación para Predicadores*, Madrid 1980. See also: G. Ma. MEDICA, *Alla Scuola di Nazaret. Maria, Maestra di vita*, Turin 1983; [P. FEHLNER, *Mater et Magistra Apostolorum*, in *Immaculata Mediatrix* 1 (1/2001) 15-95; IDEM, *Mary and Theology. Scotus Revisited*, Rensselaer, NY 1978.]

earliest times of the Christian Church: *Mary, Mother of the Church, Teacher and Queen of the Apostles.* [96]

The Pope refers to the Virgin Mary in an ecclesial and soteriological context, employing the same expressions used by Mother Agreda two and a half centuries earlier. The context in which the facts and explanations unfold is very similar.

The Pope places himself before the *"profound mystery of the inexhaustible charity of Jesus Christ,"* who on Calvary, from the Cross proclaimed His Mother as spiritual Mother of the beloved disciple, representative of the entire redeemed mankind, and in particular *"those men who had been bound to him* [with John], *by the bonds of faith."* [97] Jesus in that moment entrusted to Mary the mission of being spiritual Mother of the Church: a role of love, and of protection and of help without limit for her children.

The Pope explains with broad strokes the content of this role from its very commencement:

> *Mary Most Holy accepted with generosity of soul this singular and laborious responsibility, and began to accomplish her exalted mission in the Cenacle. She was the wonderful help and support of the newly born Church through the holiness of her example, the authority of her counsels, the sweetness of her consolation, and the efficacy of her fervent prayer, showing herself truly to be Mother of the Church and Teacher and Queen of the Apostles.* [98]

---

96 Leo XIII, Encyclical *Adiutricem populi* (September 2, 1895), in H. Marin, *Doctrina Pontificia*, IV, Documentos Marianos, Madrid 1954, n. 426.

97 Leo XIII, cit., n. 426.

98 *Ibid.*

These are the points which Mother Agreda sets in relief in her *MCG* when she describes these ineffable moments in the life of Mary: ardent love of the Mother for her divine Son, love of the Mother for her adopted sons, spiritual communion of life with the Apostles in the Cenacle, help to the newly born Church with her love, her holiness of life, her faith, her counsels, her prayers...

What can be concluded from this comparison?... A mariology based on these principles, nourished by these ideas and enlightened by these arguments coinciding with the teaching of documents of the living Magisterium of the Church, cannot be incompatible with that of a Council such as Vatican II, which is and which represents the entire Church. This is my conviction, resting as well on other, like documentation, also to be kept in mind, because these are the documents which define the orientation of contemporary mariology and which are fully in agreement with that of Mother Agreda.

Pope Paul VI, more than qualified to be the first authoritative interpreter of the mariology of Vatican II, *already* foreshadows some important aspects of this theme, principally in his brief Apostolic Exhortation *Signum Magnum* (May 13, 1967). [99]

But it was above all Pope John Paul II who most often referred to the "Magisterium" of the Mother of Jesus in relation to the Apostles, and has offered a theological explanation of her activity and of her mission in this paschal period of the Church. In various documents, of diverse character, he has alluded to the rich theological and spiritual content which frames this period in the life of Mary as Mother of the Church.

---

99 PAUL VI, Apostolic Exhortation *Signum Magnum*, May 13, 1967: AAS 59 (1967) 467-469. [This Exhortation is closely linked to the teaching ministry of Mary at Fatima.]

To evaluate the teaching of the Pope on this point – and still more to interpret the activity of Mary – one must take account of the intimate relationship which he assigns to the mystery of the Incarnation and the paschal mysteries, in reference both to their content and to the structure of the mysteries so related. [100] On this premise he then teaches that the maternal role of Mary does not only consist in conceiving, begetting and giving her Son to the light by the work of the Holy Spirit. Like other mothers she nursed, she fed, and she educated Him. Mary, says the Pope, "was the instructress of her Son, who was Son of God." For this reason God bestowed on her appropriate and singular graces.

The Pope projects his thought concerning the historic Christ, the Son of God on the Mystical Christ, the Church, and on the first Christian Community of Jerusalem, comprising the Mother of Jesus, His friends and disciples and a group of pious women.

In those first days of the Church, says the Pope, "Mary maintained a 'discrete' presence." But the function which she discharged in the primitive Community, and the command which she carried out, in the very words of the Pope, "took on notable importance" for various reasons. [101] She exercised her maternal role, as "guide of the Community," and "also in educating the disciples of the Lord in that Community and in her constant communication with God. Thus, she

---

[100] JOHN PAUL II, Encyclical *Redemptoris Mater* (25 March, 1987), 24. [Abbreviated hereafter as *RM*.] To stress the importance of this consideration the Pope indicates precisely that *the person present in these two moments is Mary*: **Mary at Nazareth and Mary in the Cenacle of Jerusalem** (*RM* 24) [author's emphasis]. In both cases her presence was *discrete, but essential*.

[101] JOHN PAUL II, Allocution, September 6, 1995: *Presence of Mary at the beginning of the Church*.

became instructress of the Christian people in prayer and in encounter with God." [102]

This activity included, as is obvious, a magisterial role, not merely one of model. Mary brought this formative activity to its high point in the primitive Community, realizing it as Teacher of the faithful, and of the Apostles. John Paul II is very specific here, and in basics along the same line of thought as Mother Agreda.

This is by no means the only document which can be adduced as proof in favor of the *MCG* on this point. John Paul II refers to other particular aspects in explanation of the sense and import of the presence of Mary among the Apostles, during the days around the Ascension of the Lord and Pentecost. He admits that the sacred books contain no special affirmations about Mary after the drama of Calvary. But at the same time he says that it is very important to know how she participated in the life of the primitive Community and in steadfast prayer. [103]

The Pope distinguishes here two moments or functions in the activity of the Mother of Jesus: a) *participate* in the life of the community; and b) *remain* in steadfast prayer. Her presence among the disciples of her Son was *discrete*, but *essential*. [104] Her presence enjoyed the same value and the same importance – we mean here in a proportionate or relational way, precisely as Mother Agreda intends this in reference to the collaboration of Mary in the redemption – as did her presence at Nazareth and her participation in the mystery of the Incarnation: the value of an *essential* presence.

102 *Ibid.*

103 JOHN PAUL II, Allocution, December 9, 1998. This manner of thinking already opens the door to, and in a certain way justifies the work of Mother Agreda, whose objective is to fill in the blanks of the sacred books with human events and explanations of the life of Mary.

104 JOHN PAUL II, *RM*, 24.

In the Encyclical *Mother of the Redeemer* John Paul II interprets the meaning of this presence as a specifically maternal function: as the virginal Mother of the Son of God. *"Already at the very beginning of the Church,"* he says, *"at the start of that long pilgrimage of faith, on Pentecost in Jerusalem, Mary was present with all those who made up the seed of the new Israel. She was present in their midst, as an exceptional witness of the mystery of Christ."* [105]

The Pope qualifies the "presence" of Mary as a maternal presence, which includes or embraces the role of being guide, model and exceptional witness. How should one understand this category of "exceptional witness?" We can reply by taking note of other documents of the same Pope.

Mary was "witness," because with her exercise of faith she confirmed the faith in the disciples of her Son. And also, because she explained orally and clarified for them certain truths or mysteries of faith which she alone could know by way of eye witness. In confirmation of this the Pope cites a concrete instance: the virginal conception of Jesus and the annunciation of the Angel, when he writes: Mary, precisely Mary, *"is the origin of the revelation of the mystery of the virginal conception by work of the Holy Spirit."* [106]

More recently, almost contemporaneously with the composition of my essay, Pope John Paul II reaffirmed this in a document of notable importance for reflection on the *magisterium of the Virgin Mary* during the different stages of her life, especially at the commencement of the Church. The context of the Pontiff's comments is one identical with that in which Mother Agreda writes and gives expression to her

---

[105] JOHN PAUL II, *RM*, 27. Further on, in a parallel text in n. 41, he adds: *"After the events of the Resurrection and of the Ascension Mary, entering with the Apostles into the Cenacle to await Pentecost, remained present there as Mother of the glorified Lord."*

[106] JOHN PAUL II, Allocution: *The maternal Face of Mary*, September 13, 1995.

convictions. The testimony of the Pope in this case is a clear confirmation of what the Venerable Authoress of the *MCG* teaches.

In the Apostolic Letter: *Rosarium Virginis Mariae* (October 16, 2002), in the section where the Pope explains the role which Mary plays in the various mysteries of her divine Son, those forming the framework of the Rosary, and precisely in the first chapter of that section, when treating of *contemplating Christ with Mary*, there the Pope analyzes various problems and aspects of contemplation, and dedicates a special paragraph to *understanding Christ with Mary* (n. 14). He proposes and considers Jesus Christ as supreme Teacher, Revealer and Revelation itself, who can give us light and help us *understand Him* better.

Referring to the Virgin Mary and turning his attention to Her, he asks: *What teacher could be more professional than Mary?... Among creatures no one more than She knows Christ better, no one could introduce us, as His Mother can, to a profound knowledge of His mystery.* [107]

One of the first manifestations of the *magisterium* of Mary, apart from other exercises and activities in relation to her Son and to the mysteries of His infancy, occurred in Cana of Galilee, during the nuptial festivities of friends, when Mary noticed that the supply of wine had given out and then said to the servants at the banquet: *Do whatever He tells you to do* (Jn 2:5). And the Pope adds this precise and especially significant commentary:

> *...we can imagine how* [Mary] *discharged this duty with the disciples after the Ascension of Jesus, when she remained with them awaiting the Holy Spirit, and when she comforted them during their first mission. To recall with Mary the scenes of the Rosary is as it were to attend*

107 JOHN PAUL II, Apostolic Letter *Rosarium Virginis Mariae*, n. 13.

the "school" of Mary to learn about Christ, to penetrate His secrets, to understand His message. [108]

In all this Mary exercised a true magisterium over the Apostles, instructing them on certain mysteries of the infancy of her Son. And she exercised this magisterium as Mother of Jesus. For this reason the presence of Mary in the beginnings of the Church, as Mother, Teacher and exemplar of the faithful is stressed in paschal tide, after the Resurrection of her Son. She was the exceptional witness and unique Teacher of the Apostles.

A detailed and in-depth analysis of the teaching of John Paul II in this context could surface new matrices for the comportment and activity which the Mother of Jesus exercised in the apostolic Community. For it is beyond question that the Apostles as pillars of the Church lived and felt in their inmost being, not only their own dignity and authority, but also a simple and respectful attitude of veneration for and spiritual filiation to the Mother of their Risen Master. To that Mother, Jesus Himself had already commended them: *Behold thy Mother...* Thus, they connaturally showed to her sentiments of love and aspired to imitate her virtues, and to listen to the words from her lips and the accounts of the

---

108 *Ibid.*, n. 14. For the Pope the *magisterium* of Mary is not an isolated phenomenon. It is an inherent function of her dignity and of her continuous, daily solicitude as spiritual Mother of the Church. Here he speaks of the "School of Mary," which would seem to suggest that after the Ascension of the Lord She exercised the role of true Teacher in the primitive Church and for the primitive Christian communities. [Since beginning his Pontificate POPE BENEDICT XVI has referred twice to the relation between the Apostles and Mary as Mother of the Church. In his homily for the feast of the Chair of St. Peter, February 22, 2006, he remarked in illustration of the relation between the petrine and marian principles of the Church that the Chair of St. Peter was first established in the Cenacle of Jerusalem on Pentecost in the presence of the Mother of God and of the Church. In the allocution of April 30, 2006, he called Mary "Mother and Teacher of the Apostles:" *Mater et Magistra Apostolorum.*]

mysteries of the infancy of their Master. The work of Mother Agreda on this point matches precisely the teaching of John Paul II.

Assuredly, from the standpoint of historical methodology this is a hypothesis yet to be demonstrated. But in the objectively valid context of a mariology of "mind and heart," such as the *Theologia mentis et cordis* of Contenson and other 17th century mariologists, it can be considered a reality. This is the kind of mariology which the Venerable Mother lived and taught, and which she passes on to us in her *MCG*. This is the mariology which the Church teaches today in making ever relevant the message of Vatican II.

In expounding these ideas, John Paul II more than once makes reference to the teaching of Vatican II, to indicate the conformity of his teaching and approach with that of the Council. In the fundamentals and the substance of this teaching on Mary, Mother and Teacher of the Church, which we are now commenting, the Pope places himself in a line of thought and moves within a schematic structure very similar, not to say identical, to that of Mother Mary of Jesus of Agreda. Is there anyone who would dare claim that this teaching of the Pope is not compatible with the mariology of Vatican II?

True, one is dealing here with a very precise and particular theme. Nonetheless, it is quite consistent and in harmony with the whole of mariology, and not just with the image which the Church hands on to us of the Mother of the Son of God.

After all that I have explained here, I believe it is legitimate to make this reflection: if the mariology of the *MCG*, on this very concrete and important point, and on many others not mentioned here, coincides with that of Pope Leo XIII and Paul VI, and in particular with that of Pope John Paul II, can anyone affirm with any minimal semblance of reason, that it is not compatible with the mariology of Vatican II?

SECTION TWO

THE MARIOLOGICAL NOTES REFLECTED IN THE *MYSTICAL CITY OF GOD*

A. INTRODUCTION

1. "Notes" of Marian Devotion = "Notes" of Catholic Mariology

Moved by the spirit of the teaching of Vatican II on the Virgin Mary, and inspired by a number of its affirmations, Pope Paul VI indicated *three* "notes" or fundamental orientations which marian devotion must possess to be authentic and pleasing to God. Here is how the Pope formulates these three notes: the Trinitarian, the Christological – which includes the pneumatological – and the Ecclesial, with its ecumenical dimension. [109]

These "notes" by which a marian pastoral activity is critiqued have an application throughout mariology. Some contemporary mariologists have in part already incorporated these into their expositions, adding a biblical note and setting the pneumatological in relief. [110] These norms, among others,

---

[109] Cf. PAUL VI, *MC*, 25-29.

[110] Cf. D. BERTETTO, *Maria, la Serva del Signore. Mariologia*. Naples 1988. The author structures his "mariology" according to the norms of Vatican II, which in a certain way include those of Paul VI in relation to devotion. See Vatican II, *Optatum totius*, 16.

serve to discern the authenticity of a mariology from the point of view of its content, and to evaluate its methodology.

Under this aspect, the mariology of the *Mystical City of God* must be considered as one of the most complete and positive within the history of Spanish mariology in the 17th century. In the face of this affirmation neither the unfortunate censure of the Faculty of Theology of the University of Paris nor the accusations of certain opponents before the tribunal of the Spanish Inquisition hold any value whatsoever. Her accusers neither knew nor utilized the true interpretive key to this singular work. They employed a key adequate for reading systematic theology as though equally adequate for understanding a historical and spiritual work of mariology (which it is not), and so caricatured the structures and principles of the latter.

Today, all the arguments and doctrinal fencing employed by its accusers against the work of Mother Agreda have been rendered irrelevant and reduced to nothing. None of the proposed difficulties has any grounds in reality: neither in the doctrine of the *MCG*, nor in the field of biblical exegesis, nor in that of doctrinal mariology. The special Commission set up in Rome to examine this work, admitted in 1999, as we have noted above, that the work contains no true doctrinal errors, and that absolutely nothing taught by the work is to be considered a "heresy." This admission suffices for taking a first step forward in this affair.

That first step taken, we should also take the second which is a formal analysis of the *MCG* in relation to those coordinates and general lines which give life and support the frame of the mariological organism. The *notes* just referred to above are, as it were, the very life breath of mariology, the elements conferring on its structure an inner cohesion, and translating its content into lessons of ever permanent interest. For this reason, perhaps, the work of Mother Agreda, after three and a half centuries of history, not only has not suffered the effects of age, but also with a certain timelessness has continued to stimulate great interest among contemporary readers.

2. Three "Notes" Basic to Mariology

According to the commentary of Pope Paul VI, the three "notes," which must be present in marian devotion for it to be authentic, notes we have applied to mariology, summarize the spirit of the teaching of Vatican II on the mystery of the Mother of God. This teaching constitutes the foundation of true marian piety, and is at the same time source of the principles which must govern the articulation of mariology, and animate its contents.

It is evident that all mariology, grounded in these principles and reflecting these characteristic notes, can be compatible with the mariology elaborated by Vatican II, if such mariology subscribes to the Council's true doctrinal content. All the more so is this true, if the basics coincide with the thought of the Council, and with its fundamental orientations, and if certain forms of expression, including terminology, coincide with the Council's, this after the passage and accretions of more that three centuries of history.

Now the fact is that there exist between the marian doctrine of the *MCG* and the marian text of Vatican II many coincidences of this kind: identity of teaching on and of forms of expression for the most basic themes, and on some themes coincidence quite particular and significant; for example: in the *consensus* or consent given by the Virgin to the message of the Angel during the Annunciation, and the soteriological value of the Mother's concerns for her Son during His infancy: *begetting Him, feeding Him…*, as we shall see further on.

In relation to the foregoing we may formulate this axiomatic principle to be illustrated in the commentary to follow: "*The mariology of the* Mystical City of God *is fully compatible, as regards its doctrinal content, with that articulated in Vatican II.*" Included in this axiom is the coincidence of that mariology with the teaching of Vatican II on the most important and most fundamental doctrinal themes of mariology: biblical mariology, predestination of Mary and its content, Immaculate Conception and preservation of the Virgin from original sin and from all sin; concept, value and dignity of the divine-virginal Maternity; collaboration of Mary with her Son in the Redemption: in subordination to Him, yet "according to a certain proportion;" sanctity; glorious Assumption into heaven; spiritual Maternity; universal exemplarity; *Mother and Teacher of the Church*, etc.

B. DEVELOPMENT

Vatican II has given methodological orientations for the teaching of dogmatic and systematic theology, without doubt to be applied and to be extended to the very structure of such theology. Point of departure must be the study of these themes and theological truths in biblical revelation, guided by an analysis of the teaching of the Holy Fathers, both of the East and of the West. Beginning thus, one may proceed to reflect on these revealed truths in relation to other parallel questions, to be illustrated in the light of the teaching of

St. Thomas Aquinas, authorized "Master" according to the Council. [111]

This applies, therefore, to mariology. The Council did not set down concrete outlines for the structuring of theology, or mariology. It preferred to safeguard the contents of the truths, which must integrate and form part of the teaching.

In a certain manner the orientations distinctive of the Council are also the basis and foundation of the lines and configuration which the articulation of a scientific mariology must manifest. The norms set out by Pope Paul VI for the exercise of marian devotion and which can be extended to

---

111 Cf. Vatican II, *Optatam totius*, 16: "*The theological disciplines should be taught in the light of faith under the direction of the Magisterium of the Church... Dogmatic theology should be taught in such wise that biblical themes are first proposed, to be followed by an explanation of the contribution of the Fathers of the Church of East and West... The remaining theological disciplines must be similarly renewed by means of a living contact with the mystery of Christ...*" [Vatican II clearly reaffirms the theological authority of St. Thomas, but it does not deny, as Leo XIII did not deny, the position of St. Bonaventure (and implicitly Bl. John Duns Scotus who develops and perfects the theological work of the Seraphic Doctor) in the theological world, set on a par with that of St. Thomas by Pope Sixtus V when he declared St. Bonaventure a primary Doctor of the Church (1587, *Triumphantis Hierusalem*). The *MCG* of Mother Agreda does indeed reflect the distinctive theses of Franciscan, and in particular scotistic mariology, but this hardly justifies accusing her of being anti-thomistic, anymore than reflection of characteristic features of thomistic mariology makes one anti-scotistic. Either way her mariology, in its basics, coincides with that of the Church. Accusations of anti-thomism against the Venerable seem to have their origin in the disgraceful censure of the Sorbonne in 1696, a censure reflecting not impartial assessment, but a triple bias quite potent in late 17th century France: theologically, a Jansenistic and anti-marian bias; academically, an anti-scholastic bias, particularly in its scotistic form; politically an anti-Spanish bias. On each count the *MCG* was a prime target. For the rest, in his Christmas address to the members of the Roman Curia, December 22, 2005, POPE BENEDICT XVI insists on interpreting Vatican II, not in terms of a break in tradition and the inauguration of a different theology (and so by implication mariology), but always on the premise of perfect identity in essentials with the preceding theological (and so also mariological) tradition. Cf. *L'Osservatore Romano*, December 23, 2005, pp. 4-5.]

the teaching of mariology, fill this methodological vacuum in the conciliar text.

It may be noted here that we are not dealing with methodological norms in the strict sense. Rather these lines correspond to various essential aspects of the mystery of Mary. They must be clearly reflected in a theological exposition and explanation, which is objective and fully realistic. Without this, the image of this mystery will suffer impoverishment and some of the features of this mystery pertaining to its essential configuration will remain veiled. Certainly these norms can favorably and positively influence mariological method.

The "notes," indicated by Paul VI, seek to set in relief the relation of the mystery of Mary to this threefold orientation. Mary, by the very fact of her being Mother of the Son of God, assumes a special relation to the Trinity and in particular to each one of the divine persons (Trinitarian "note"). Further, a special and most singular relation with the Son of God made Man, with Jesus Christ, is hers (christological "note"); and so a relation also with the Church, mystical body of Christ, because her life and mission unfold within the history of salvation (Ecclesial "note").

Under this last heading one can deepen the relation of Mary with the Church by introducing a number of additional considerations. The Church maintains that her own source and origin is the Trinity, as Vatican II teaches: *Ecclesia de Trinitate...* Mary also finds her source and origin in the Trinity. The *MCG* can illustrate still other aspects of this relation of Mary with the Church: as *Mother, Teacher, Queen, Exemplar...*

1. The *Mystical City of God*, a "Trinitarian" Mariology

a. *Trinitarian mariology of Vatican II*

The mariology of Vatican II possesses a dimension and structure truly Trinitarian. Commentators have set this in relief, and this has been stressed by Msgr. G. Philips, redactor of chapter VIII of the Constitution on the Church, *Lumen Gentium: "The All Holy Virgin Mary, Mother of God, in the mystery of Christ and of the Church."* The very fact of so contextualizing the mystery of Mary in the *historia salutis* is a proof of this orientation. For it is the divine Trinity which gives origin to and presides over this history and its entire unfolding. The Trinity is the source and the origin of the mysteries of salvation: Incarnation, Passion and Death of Jesus, Resurrection-Pentecost, and the Church *de Trinitate*. [112]

Mary is also a mystery of salvation. Paul VI states, as we have observed above, that she forms an *essential* part of the mystery of salvation. [113]

On the other hand, the marian chapter of the Constitution *Lumen Gentium* begins and ends with a reference to the three divine Persons united in charity. [114] This gives to the entire Constitution a marian matrix, in harmony with the origin of the Church *de Trinitate*. In consonance with this, the text of the Council on the Virgin Mary, from its very start, places in relief the essential and more characteristic Trinitarian features of her figure by use of a phrase classic in the marian tradition of the Church: Mary, *"Mother of the Son of God, and for this reason beloved Daughter of the Father and*

---

112 Cf. G. PHILIPS, *La Vierge au II Concile du Vatican et l'avenir de la mariologie*, cit., pp. 48-49.

113 See above, note 13.

114 Cf. G. PHILIPS, *op. cit.*, 48, 50-54.

Sanctuary of the Holy Spirit." [115] In accord with this a number of contemporary mariologists have given their mariologies a Trinitarian structure, so rejoining the 17th century Spanish mariological school. [116]

b. The Trinitarian mariology of the Mystical City of God

1) The mariology of Mother Agreda is fundamentally Trinitarian in character. It is at once a conclusion deduced both from the internal analysis of many chapters of the *MCG*, and from the structural organization which the Venerable Authoress has in explanation of the mystery of the Immaculate, Mother of the Son of God, as well as the core principle guiding that exposition. By means of this analysis we also become aware of many doctrinal coincidences, even in doctrinal terminology, between the text of the Council and a number of formulations of the *MCG*.

To establish and clarify our basic affirmation it suffices to take note of the general structure which Mother Agreda gives her work, and its title: *Mystical City of God*, which in a certain manner determines the lines of its entire content. This title is a symbol, of biblical inspiration, since medieval times

---

115 Vatican II, *Lumen Gentium*, 53.

116 The distinguished Salesian mariologist, DOMENICO BERTETTO, has done just this in his important work: *Maria, la serva del Signore. Mariologia,* cit. He divides the work into two parts: *positive and systematic.* The systematic part comprises four principal sections: 1. Mary and the divine person of the Father; 2. Mary and the divine person of the Son; 3. Mary and the divine person of the Holy Spirit. The fourth section deals with one of the notes signaled by Paul VI: the ecclesial note or Mary in the mystery of the Church.

The Trinitarian structure in 17th century Spanish mariology can be observed in various authors, all independent of one another: Pedro de Bivero, José de la Cerda and Silvestre Saavedra. See my study: *La Virgin María y el Mistero de la Trinidad en la mariología del siglo XVII,* in PAMI, *De Trinitatis Mysterio et Maria,* vol. I, Vatican City 2004, pp. 361-406.

expressly acknowledged as part of the marian tradition of the Church. Mystically and spiritually Mary is the city built and erected by God, one and triune, as throne and living abode of the three divine Persons, with whom, on grounds of her predestination as the Mother of God, enjoys special relations.

For this reason Mother Agreda at the beginning of her work designates the All Holy Virgin by a formulary which St. Francis of Assisi made popular: *Daughter of the Eternal Father, Spouse of the Holy Spirit, and Mother of true Light* [the Son]. [117] This was the title, a kind of emblem or praise, which the Most Blessed Trinity inscribed in letters of finest gold on the white and shining vestment of the child Mary, as she was consecrated to divine service in the temple of Jerusalem. It is a way of expressing the Immaculate Conception of Mary, full of grace. In our day Vatican II made use of the same formulary in slightly different form, substituting "sanctuary" for "spouse" of the Holy Spirit.

On another occasion the Venerable Mary employs the same phrase to demonstrate the very singular love "which the Most Blessed Trinity has for the Mother of the Son, Daughter of the Father and Spouse of the Holy Spirit." [118]

---

117 *MCG*, Lib. II, ch. 2, n. 435, p. 188 [I, 341].

118 *MCG*, Lib. II, ch. 14, n. 622, p. 264 [I, 481]. With the same meaning and in similar form she uses the same expression in n. 630, p. 267 [I, 487]; n. 769, p. 320 [I, 584]; and in the introduction to part 2, n. 22, p. 344 [II, 15-16]. [Some have held that since the Council deliberately refrained from using the title "Spouse of the Holy Spirit" for the Immaculate Virgin and chose always to use "sanctuary" in this context to avoid possible misinterpretations along the lines of a pagan "theogamy," therefore mariologies such as the *MCG*, and in general those inspired by St. Francis of Assisi, popularizer, if not author of the title "Spouse of the Holy Spirit" (from the Antiphon for his *Office of the Passion*), are not fully in accord with the mariology of Vatican II. But as J. GALOT, *Marie, Mere et Coredemptrice* (Paris 2005) notes in the first part of this work dealing with the mystery of virginal maternity, the claimed opposition between the two titles is a pseudo-problem. Spouse accents the unique bond of love between

2)   The entire *MCG* has a Trinitarian dimension, because it was composed, according to the testimony of the Venerable Authoress herself, "*in the light of the Most Blessed Trinity*," which like a seal or logo distinguishes and identifies all its pages. [119] We should have to examine all the mysteries of the life of the Virgin Mary, to form a fully accurate estimate of the importance which the Authoress gives to the presence of the Trinity in the Virgin's life and in her mission, described in thousands of ways: the action of the Trinity in her life and of each of the divine Persons according to those distinctive features which characterize and identify him.

The mystery of the Trinity confers a certain unity on the *MCG:* it was the Trinity which chose and declared Mary Queen and Mistress of all creatures, and which placed a crown of stars upon the head of Her, whom all should venerate and proclaim with the honored title of *Mother of God.* [120]

3)   In the *MCG* the description of the mystery of the Incarnation, the "wonder of the ages," is totally Trinitarian in character beginning with the mission of the Archangel St. Gabriel to announce to the Immaculate Virgin the mystery which the Holy Trinity would accomplish in her. This is

---

the Trinity and Mary, appropriated to the Holy Spirit; sanctuary stresses the effect of that love in Mary as term of the Spirit's mission *ad extra*. St. Bonaventure and Ubertino almost always use the title sanctuary, whereas most of the other great representatives of the Franciscan tradition in mariology, of which Mother Agreda is an integral part: from Conrad of Saxony down to contemporary figures such as St. Maximilian M. Kolbe, prefer the title spouse, because it is so intimately connected with the mystery of the Immaculate Conception and the joint predestination of Christ and Mary. But they do not thereby exclude the title "sanctuary."]

119 *MCG*, Part 2, n. 25, p. 345 [II, 17].

120 *MCG*, Lib. III, n. 92, p. 381 [II, 80]; see n. 103, p. 394 [II, 87-88].

clear from the very title of chapter 10 of Book III, [121] and in the description of the realization of this mystery. [122]

Through the graces and most abundant supernatural gifts which she had received from heaven, Mary as Immaculate in her conception and chosen to be Mother of the Son of God by the power of the Holy Spirit, was "*made heaven, temple and abode of the Most Holy Trinity.*" [123] This phrase and this description remind me of what Vatican II says concerning the mystery of the Annunciation, where it describes the figure of Mary as *full of all the gifts* appropriate to her office, totally *holy and immune of all sin,* as *formed and made a new creature by the Holy Spirit.* [124]

Finally, Mary assented to the message of the Angel. Her "yes," or her obedience to the will of the Father: *Be it done to me according to thy word* was the beginning of our redemption. And it was the Most Holy Trinity which accepted the role of Mary, the Mother of Jesus as "*assistant to her Son in the work of redemption.*" [125]

4) These testimonials are sufficient to impress on us the Trinitarian dimension of the *MCG*. This dimension is

---

[121] "*Chapter 10. The Most Blessed Trinity dispatches St. Gabriel the Archangel to announce the good news to Mary Most Holy that she has been chosen to be Mother of God.*" MCG, Lib. III, p. 387 [II, 92].

[122] *MCG*, Lib. III, ch. 11-12, n. 123-157, pp. 392-407 [II, 100-128].

[123] *MCG*, Lib. III, n. 140, p. 399 [II, 113].

[124] Vatican II, *Lumen Gentium*, 56.

[125] *MCG*, Lib. III, n. 151, p. 404 [II, 122-123]. Since the Middle Ages it has been commonplace to contemplate the mystery of the Annunciation from a Trinitarian perspective. One can also appreciate, then, a certain parallelism between the fundamental features of the description which Mother Agreda draws and that of the *Arbor Vitae* of Ubertino of Casale, who says that Mary was then recognized as *Spouse of God the Father, Mother and Associate of his Son, and Sanctuary of the Holy Spirit. A sanctuary and most lovely temple of the entire Trinity, Queen and Mistress of the Angels.* UBERTINO OF CASALE, *Arbor Vitae*, Lib. I, ch. 9. See *MCG*, Lib. III, ch. 11, n. 399 [II, 113], and pp. 392-399 [II, 100-113].

universal, because Mother Agreda inserts the life of Mary within the "history of salvation:" in the *historia salutis*, whose origin is the Holy Trinity, and whose unfolding is realized under its beneficent action.

The Trinitarian character in the *MCG* extends to its content, and is revealed more concretely in certain phrases and expressions identical with those of Vatican II.

From another point of view the Venerable Authoress is perfectly conversant with and wisely applies on many occasions and with full theological acumen this basic principle of Trinitarian theology: "*the works of God ad extra are common to the entire Trinity.*"

2.   The *Mystical City of God*, a Christological Mariology

a.   The christological "note"

The figure of Jesus Christ, the Word of God, the Son of the Father made flesh, is seen at the point of departure of the *Mystical City of God*, as object of the predestination of Mary conjointly with the mystery of the Incarnation. He stands in the center, as the very crown of her doctrine on the Mother of God and collaborator in the work of redemption of the human race; He is present when she reaches the goal of her life, the glorification in body and soul of the Mother and Queen at the side of her risen and glorified Son.

Pope Paul VI, inspired by Vatican II and following its orientation, reflects thus on the christological dimension of marian piety and the centrality of Christ in the life of the Church. That centrality also finds full application in mariology, and concretely is found in the *MCG*. At the same time this Pope offers us a guideline useful for a better understanding of this aspect of mariology reflected in the pages of the *MCG*.

In effect says the Pope: "*In the Virgin Mary all is relative to Christ, and all is dependent on Him. God the Father has chosen her from all eternity as the All Holy Mother, and has adorned her with gifts of the Holy Spirit not bestowed on anyone else.*" [126]

This text is particularly significant for us. Mother Agreda considers the Virgin in relation to Christ. Precisely for this reason and because she was His Mother according to nature and the spirit, she affirms a number of privileges bestowed on the Mother, in analogy with and in relation to those of her Son, in particular the paschal privileges: her glorious Assumption, her glorification in heaven, her mediation and intercession in the life of grace, her Queenship... Her collaboration in the redemption was dependent on that of her Son, and proportionately similar to the redemptive action of the Redeemer.

b. The christological "note" in the MCG

1) In addition to all this, one is well advised to take account of how in the first place the *MCG* describes the predestination of the Virgin Mary, conjointly with the mystery of the Incarnation, to be Mother of the Son of God and collaborator with Him in the redemption. This is the backbone of the structure of the *MCG*, or as it were the trunk of the tree, from which extend the branches covering and adorning it.

Hereafter in the *MCG* Mary appears in everything totally relative to Christ. Nothing which the Venerable Authoress ascribes to Mary has even the shadow of autonomy. All the graces, all the supernatural and natural gifts, the perfections and privileges bestowed on her, her very existence, speak of a relation to and depend on the mystery of the

---

[126] PAUL VI, *MC*, 25.

Incarnation. Christ is present in one or another manner, expressly or implicitly, in all the pages of the *MCG*.

2) Vatican II, interpreting the content of the Incarnation, in regard to what pertains to the predestined Mother, asserts that the Virgin Mary, in speaking her *"yes"* of acceptance of the saving will of the Father: *Behold the handmaid of the Lord, be it done to me according to thy word* (Lk 1:38), became Mother of God, and *consecrated* her very self to the Person and work of her Son. [127]

Because of its importance for the mystery of the Incarnation, this affirmation confers a christological sense on marian doctrine. Mother Agreda does not use this expression of the Council: *she consecrated herself to the Person of her Son*. But she understands Mary's *yes* as an affirmative reply to the message of the Angel, a reply which expresses her full dedication and consecration of her person and of her life to the service of her Son, as an act of sacrificial love, in order to collaborate in the work of the redemption of men. For in that very moment and in the environment of that mystery, says the Venerable Mother, *"she offered herself in an acceptable sacrifice to serve, to nourish and feed her most sweet Son and to assist Him and cooperate, as much as it were possible to her, in the work of the redemption. And the Most Holy Trinity accepted her and marked her as helper and associate by this very sacrament."* [128]

3) *Nourish, feed, serve* a child are natural functions, inherent in every mother. They are functions which surround the obligations of a mother for her child: to care for him, to feed him... But in this exceptional case these roles were raised to a higher plane. These acts in the Virgin Mary were conscious acts of love and of obedience to the Father's will.

---

127 Vatican II, *Lumen Gentium*, 56.

128 *MCG*, Lib. III, n. 151, p. 404 [II, 122].

Mother Agreda assesses and interprets them as collaboration of the Mother with the Son in the Redemption, an interpretation ratified by Vatican II, employing, let us admit it, the very same terminology. This is one more factual example of coincidence in doctrine and in forms of expression between the *MCG* and the conciliar text. The parallelism, even if brief, is perfectly plain and of highest importance:

MOTHER AGREDA	VATICAN II
"Offering herself as an acceptable sacrifice in His service, to nourish and feed her Son... And to assist and to cooperate with Him...in the work of the redemption." [129]	"In conceiving Christ, in begetting Him, feeding Him, offering Him to the Father... she cooperated in an absolutely unique manner in the work of the Savior." [130]

4) The christological character of the mariology of the *MCG* is particularly evident in the chapters devoted to explaining the presence and the spiritual participation of the Mother in the Passion of her Son. [131] In few works of mariology overall, and in her times in no other, was the theology of the Virgin as associated in the suffering of Jesus and as sharer of those sufferings so amply explained.

In effect, the Virgin shared in certain mysteries and certain moments, offering herself to the Father as an unbloody sacrifice, suffering in spirit what her Son suffered in his flesh. She suffered this in her heart. The saving value of her actions and of her suffering derives from the infinite merits of her Son, universal Savior.

This doctrine and these sentiments permeate a great part of Mother Agreda's mariology, converting it into a true mariology of mind and heart: *mentis et cordis*, which as far as

---

129 *Ibid.*

130 Vatican II, *Lumen Gentium*, 61.

131 *MCG*, Lib. VI, ch. 12-25, pp. 930-1071 [III, 472-726].

its contents are concerned, is today a general teaching of the Church.

5) There is still more: Mother Agreda has incorporated into her mariology an important chapter, which we may classify as a "paschal mariology," one which reinforces and sets in greater relief its christological aspect. Until her time, mariological manuals gave scant or no attention to the presence and role of Mary in relation to the paschal mysteries: Resurrection, Ascension and Pentecost... Mother Agreda, as I see it, has the good sense of suggesting and including a series of themes relevant to the Risen Christ, which fill in the blanks and break the silence of written Revelation.

The principle grounding this activity is the unbreakable association of Mother and Son in the work of salvation and her vital and spiritual union with Him in these mysteries, which are also mysteries of the Church, as we shall see further on.

This consideration reinforces the christological aspects and character of her mariology. This chapter might perhaps be considered as a bridge effecting passage to the study of the mysteries of marian eschatology in chronological order. These are the mysteries such as the Assumption and Queenship of Mary which also entail a profound christological meaning.

6) Mary is entirely relative to Christ and dependent on Him. Fully cognizant of this postulate, Mother Agreda, in treating these paschal mysteries, takes the Risen Christ for this reason as the center of reference for all her reflections. With such a methodology the sense of the saving association of the Mother with her divine Son stands out more.

Leaving aside some events, which in the context of this chapter, the Venerable Authoress recounts as historical facts – events which can be explained taking account of the finality of hagiographical works in the baroque age – and fixing our attention on the doctrinal content of the *MCG*, we may conclude that here the figure of Jesus Christ occupies a central place, and illumines all the mysteries of the life of His Mother, the Immaculate Virgin, who from her predestination was associated with Him in the work of salvation: in the times of prophecy, during her life on earth, and in the paschal and post-paschal mysteries.

7)   Finally, an attentive reader of the *MCG* can easily discover throughout her pages the line of thought which crisscrosses the entire work. That line of thought is the element, or leit-motif determining the essentially christological character of her work. It is the very reality of Jesus Christ, who is focal point and center of convergence for all Mother Agreda asserts and explains about the Virgin Mary. For the Virgin is above all and from every perspective the Mother of the Son of God. For this reason she is essentially and totally relative to her Son.

The Venerable Mother never overlooks this basic reality in anything she expounds and affirms concerning the Virgin of Nazareth. In brilliant or in veiled form, the image of Jesus Christ always appears in the backdrop of the important themes she explains in her book. For this reason the *MCG* is a work eminently christological.

Besides this, another idea is found in the work of the Venerable Mother, a parallel line of thought met on all her pages, which as it were parallels the above-mentioned. On occasion she places it to the forefront in her exposition. This is the principle of *association* of Mary with Christ, of Mother with Son in the work of redemption.

Mother Agreda offers a quite complete doctrinal synthesis on the Virgin Mary as Associate of the Redeemer, covering all its major features, from the joint decree of predestination with the mystery of the Incarnation of the Son of God until consummation of this association in the redemption with the death and resurrection of the Redeemer. We can affirm that in the thought of Mother Agreda, this role forms an essential part of the image of the Immaculate Virgin, who was predestined Mother of the Son of God, so as to be collaborator with Him in the redemption of the human race.

In her work Mother Agreda has sufficiently set in relief all these elements, which constitute the object and content of Mary's predestination conjointly with Christ, maintaining a perfect balance between what pertains to the saving plans of God and what pertains their realization in time. For this reason the *MCG* can be considered among works of its kind one of the more important from the standpoint of the christological "note" of mariology.

By way of complement, Pope Paul VI adds to the christological "note" of marian devotion another "note" to be classified as *pneumatological*, i.e., one guaranteeing that in devotional and doctrinal attitudes there is given *an adequate prominence to the Person and work of the Holy Spirit.* [132]

From this point of view we must consider the *MCG* a pioneer and leader in books on mariology, and in works dealing with the Mother of God. I cannot make an exhaustive evaluation of all mariological writings of Mother Agreda's epoch, because I have not yet consulted every book. But it is certainly fair to say that the *MCG* is one of the most important books of this type ever composed.

The Venerable Authoress has a sufficiently ample exposition, lucid and convincing, of the presence and action appropriated to the Holy Spirit – she is ever aware of the theological principle according to which all the works of God *ad extra* are common to the Trinity, a principle cited on various occasions – in the predestination and in the Immaculate

---

132 PAUL VI, *MC*, 26.

Conception of the Virgin Mary. [133] This is equally the case in the virginal conception of the Son of God, [134] in her holiness and in the bestowal of the gifts of the Holy Spirit, [135] in the visit which Mary made to her cousin Elizabeth, [136] in the annunciation of the Angel to St. Joseph in sleep, as St. Matthew recounts, [137] in the mysteries of the infancy and in the description of the Last Supper and institution of the Eucharist, [138] in certain moments of the Passion and in the description of the days of glory and the apparitions of the Risen Christ, and in the mystery of Pentecost. [139]

One must ponder the importance of this activity of the Spirit and of this contribution Mother Agreda makes to a question which aroused no theological interest until our times. In the context of ancient mariology, the *MCG* is the work which treats most fully and systematically the relations of the Virgin Mary with the Holy Spirit.

3. The *Mystical City of God* and its Ecclesial "Note"

a. Preamble

1) Since the patristic era the Virgin Mary has been considered figure, type and icon of the Church. Vatican II cites St. Ambrose as an authority holding her to be such in the order of faith, of charity and of perfect union with Christ. [140]

---

133 *MCG*, Lib. I, ch. 15, pp. 97-102 [I, 173-183].

134 *MCG*, Lib. III, ch. 11. pp. 393 ff. [II, 100-115].

135 *MCG*, Lib. II, ch. 13 ff., pp. 253 ff. [I, 462 ff.].

136 *MCG*, Lib. III, ch. 16, pp. 402 ff. [II, 162 ff.].

137 *MCG*, Lib. III, ch. 15, pp. 399 ff. [II, 154 ff.].

138 *MCG*, Lib. VI, n. 1183, pp. 919 and ff. [III, 430 ff.].

139 *MCG*, Lib. VII, ch. 5, n. 1153 and ff. [IV, 83 ff.].

140 Vatican II, *Lumen Gentium*, 63.

This typology, however, was not explained or developed theologically. For St. Ambrose and many authors of the ecclesiastical tradition the concept of type was the equivalent of "exemplar," "model." So also, Vatican II seems to have understood this typology in its very summary explanation of it in relation to virginity and motherhood. Along this line, says the Council, the Most Holy Virgin anticipates the mystery of the Church in a unique way, both as Virgin and as Mother. [141]

The Council does not explain the content of this terminology, nor the theological concepts which it involves. This is normal. This was not its task. Nor did medieval authors contribute anything of interest by way of explanation, no doubt because of the preoccupation in those times with the juridical aspects of the Church. This typology seemed to have been studied mostly by Cistercian monks. Important for their testimony are two Abbots: Guerric and Aelred, who explain with precision the ecclesial typology of the Mother of Jesus, to whose names may be added the great Franciscan Doctor, St. Bonaventure. [142]

The 16th and 17th century theologians do not abound in reflections and explanations of Mary as type and figure of the Church. "Ecclesiology" as such was not a common object of theological reflection, or when it was, these reflections were

---

141 *Ibid.*

142 Cf. ABBOT GUERRIC, *Sermo de Assumptione Beatae Mariae:* PL 185, 187-189; Abbot Aelred, *Sermo 20 in Nativitate Sanctae Mariae:* PL 195, 322-324. [All the major points of Mother Agreda, in particular the title *Mater et Magistra Apostolorum*, also *Doctrix Apostolorum*, are amply treated (although not in the form of a systematic treatise) by the Seraphic Doctor, especially in his marian discourses and scriptural commentaries. Cf. the classic study by L. Di Fonzo, *Doctrina S. Bonaventurae de universali Mediatione B. Virginis Mariae* (Romae 1938). The unique and important contribution of the *MCG* is not the novelty of the doctrine, but the inspired organization of this part of the deposit of faith, bringing it to the attention not only of pious lay-folk, but of professional theologians as well.].

centered mostly on juridical aspects and on the authority of the hierarchy. The *MCG* is one of the first works to trace a path for theological consideration of Mary in relation to the Church. Mother Agreda invokes and reflects on her as *Mother and Teacher of the Church, Teacher of the Apostles*, thus giving rise not to a juridical, but to a theological and spiritual question, whose origin and scope she proposes to determine.

2)   Mother Agreda's work served precisely as a preamble for introducing this question, which today is very familiar to us, but in the 17th century, when Mother Agreda was writing, was a novel question and a rarity, at least in the sense in which she formulates and resolves it. With these things in mind we can better understand the thought and affirmations of the Venerable Authoress, and assess her contribution to mariology on this point. Indeed, her mariology can contribute in our day to a more profound exposition of the maternal role of Mary in the Church during the apostolic age, a role which includes a magisterium in respect to the Apostles commissioned by her Son to evangelize the entire world. [143]

Let us put aside the question of the historicity of the facts which Mother Agreda presents as facts: encounters of Jesus with the just of the Old Testament, encounters with His Mother, encounters with St. Peter and with the twelve Apostles, etc. That which interests us is the content and

---

[143] The exposition which the Venerable Authoress offers of Mary, Mother and Teacher of the Church, includes affirmations of other historical facts, events occurring between the Resurrection and Pentecost, which appear to be in reference to what is reported in the Sacred Books. No one is obliged to believe these facts, nor are they necessary for the theological and spiritual explanation. Nonetheless, I still claim that they are appropriate and as to their basic historicity they might very well have happened, especially if they are considered in the light of the events and the normal conduct of life in the Apostolic Community.

doctrinal dimension which the *MCG* assigns the divine and spiritual Maternity of Mary, and her living and familiar presence in the apostolic Community constituting the body of the Church. By its presence in the world, this community, so constituted, inaugurated a new style of life in common.

b.   *Formulation of the question*

1)   Pope Paul VI describes what he calls the *"ecclesial note"* of marian devotion and what we are applying – on grounds of clear and sufficient analogy, I believe – to the structure and orientation of mariology. He writes: *"It is necessary, moreover, that exercises of piety...make perfectly clear the place occupied by Her* [Mary] *in the Church: the one highest after Christ and nearest to us..."* [144]

Recourse to fundamental concepts explained by Vatican II concerning the nature of the Church...will permit the faithful to recognize more easily the role of Mary in the mystery of the Church, and the eminent place which she occupies in the Communion of Saints. [145]

Viewed from such a perspective the *MCG* can be declared one of the works of 17th century Spanish mariology which has had the greatest influence on the people of God in making them aware of the *eminent place* which the *Virgin Mary occupies in the Communion of Saints* to which Paul VI refers. Few works have expounded with such clarity and theological sureness, as this one has, the post which Mary occupies in the mystery of salvation as "the highest after Christ and the one nearest us." It is to this to which in the steps of Vatican II, Paul VI refers. Our Lady's is the highest place after Christ in virtue of her dignity as Mother of God,

---

144 PAUL VI, *MC*, 28. Vatican II, *Lumen Gentium*, 54. Cf. PAUL VI, *Allocution* for the close of the second session of the Council, November 24, 1963: AAS 56 (1964) p. 37.

145 PAUL VI, *MC*, 28.

of her predestination, of her Immaculate Conception and her fullness of grace and other supernatural gifts; and it is the one nearest us in virtue of her spiritual maternity, and precisely in virtue of that mission which the Mother of Jesus fulfills in the ecclesial apostolic Community as Mother and Teacher of the Church, as explained above.

2) With this "ecclesial note" the *MCG* links another important idea, which re-assesses and increases the ecclesial value of the mariology of the Venerable Mary of Jesus of Agreda. In this work more than in any other, Mary is a *mystery*, who lives, obeys the will of the Father, and loves the Lord with a most pure heart. The heart of the theology of this mystery, in this instance of mariology, is the knowledge and the explanation of Mary's dispositions and of her human, womanly and supernatural sentiments... For all, such in Her, as in Jesus, holds saving value.

In this chapter on the presence and the mission of Mary in the Apostolic Community during the paschal and post-paschal tide Mother Agreda adduces many elements and many ideas to describe the spiritual dispositions of the Mother of Jesus, *Mother and Teacher of the Church*. The exercise of this spiritual maternity over the disciples of her Son, proclaimed by Jesus Himself on Calvary, produced a sheaf of dispositions and sentiments, not lacking in theological value, and placed the spiritual Mother of the Church close to all the faithful as a most excellent model and example for their life.

An ear of this sheaf was the magisterium which she exercised in the Community of the Apostles, and in groups of the primitive communities of Jerusalem, Jericho, Nazareth, Bethlehem, Bethany..., and in other families of disciples.

Mary was Mother and Teacher of the newly born Church. Her motherhood and magisterium were exercised every day and in every moment with a spiritual exemplarity which helped to strengthen the building of the Church, then taking its first steps. Mary contributed to its expansion and growth, as a Mother attends and contributes to the development of the life and to the education of her children.

There remains naught else at this point but to gather the ideas and suggestions which spontaneously arise and accompany the reading of the pages of the final section of the *MCG*. On them is the marian seal and imprint which marks the Church and has marked her since her birth. Who could doubt this reality, and the worth of the teaching of Mother Agreda on this point?

c. *The ecclesial value of the teaching of the* MCG: *Mary, Mother-Teacher of the Church*

1) While not overlooking other themes, it is nonetheless obligatory to stress this intuition of Mother Agreda, and of her doctrine about Mary, as *Mother and Teacher of the Church*. I commented above on the why, the when, and the form under which she gives these titles to the Virgin Mary, and the sense in which she intends them. They pertain to that phase of the life of Mary, chronologically following on the Resurrection of her Son, and around His glorious Ascension into heaven.

Jesus had to absent Himself visibly from His disciples, from the Church on earth to return to the Father. And it was fitting, the better to secure its permanence and facilitate its development, to set in relief and confirm the dignity and mission of His Mother, whom he had solemnly proclaimed from the Cross spiritual Mother of His disciples, and to whom He had entrusted their care. He had promised and assured them that He would remain with them until the end of the world. [146] This promise He fulfilled by the sending and the presence of the Spirit Consoler, the Holy Spirit.

On another occasion He made the same promise in these terms: *I will not leave you orphans*, informing them of His return in a proximate future: *I will return to you.* [147] Is there a reference here to the corporal presence of His Mother in their midst beginning with His Resurrection and Ascension into heaven, and to her solicitude and guidance as spiritual Mother?… Under some aspect and in some sense He must have made His disciples aware of the content and significance of the spiritual Mother whom He gave to the Church on Calvary, and have indicated the full sense of this singular and transcendental fact for the life of all His disciples.

After recounting various "miracles and favors" which the Risen Christ had done for the newly born Church, events and occurrences, which despite their lack of historical documentation, we may legitimately presume to have been real, the Most Holy Trinity made known to the heavenly Church: the Angels and Saints, the eminent place granted and the mission entrusted to the Virgin Mary in the ecclesial Community: "*Turning, the three Divine Persons directed their words to the choir of Holy Angels; and speaking with them and the rest of the just and saints, said: 'This is the Queen of all creation, in heaven and on earth; she is the Protectress of the Church, Mistress of creation,' Mother of mercy…Mother of fair love.*" [148]

Mary accepted this appointment of the eternal God, as she had accepted the Father's will at the Annunciation of the Angel. All her life is a continuation of that sublime moment of the Incarnation of the Son of God in her most pure

---

[146] Cf. Mt 28:20: "And behold, I am with you all days until the end of the world."

[147] Jn 14:18.

[148] *MCG*, Lib. VI, ch. 28, n. 1501, p. 1090 [III, n. 790, 761].

womb. Once she learned the dispositions from on high, *she humiliated herself to the dust*, and offered herself to the Lord to labor in the service of the Church, obeying the divine will.

From this point on Mary "*accepted anew the care of the evangelical Church, as loving Mother of all her children.*" From then on she renewed "*her incessant and fervent...prayers...*" [149] She consecrated herself to the service of the Church, living the fullness of the mission which her Son and the Persons of the Trinity had entrusted to her: "*She offered herself with the most prudent of reasons and most ardent of affection to labor as faithful servant in the holy Church, and obey promptly the divine will.*" [150]

2) By way of summary: all that Mother Agreda affirms and teaches in chapter 28, and all that she will say further on in part 3 of her work, as she already informs us here: – *as we shall see in the third part* – brings us to this conclusion, as it were her basic position in this question:

> *By this blessing, and by those to be conferred on Her later, Mary Most Holy was raised to an order in which she shares in the being of her Son beyond all possibility of words to explain; for by this blessing He [Christ] communicated His attributes and perfections to Her in correspondence to the ministry of Mother and Teacher of the Church and as supplying His own ministry. He elevated Her into a new state of knowledge and power, by means of which knowledge and power nothing was to be hidden from Her either of the divine mysteries or of the inmost secrets of the human heart.* [151]

---

149 MOTHER AGREDA mentions here that she will explain all this more fully further on in part 3 of her work, effectively beginning with chapter one of Book VII, pp. 1121 and ff. [IV, 29 ff.].

150 *MCG*, Lib. VI, p. 1091 [III, n. 790, 763].

151 *MCG*, Lib. VI, n. 1501, p. 1091 [III, 761 ff.]. MOTHER AGREDA here adopts a position, which might be thought questionable, concerning Mary's participation as Mother and Teacher of the Church in the being

d. The teaching of the MCG and the doctrine of the Church

1)   Mother Agreda not only does not separate the Virgin Mary from the Church, but she situates her, better than any other 17th century theologian, in the very heart of the Church, as spiritual Mother at the center of the Church's love for God and for men and as Teacher and model at the root of the Church's apostolate.   Mary as Mother of the Church is the expression and the highest manifestation of the love of Jesus Christ, as Redeemer of mankind. She is an inexhaustible fountain who receives her grace and her light from her Son, to be communicated to the members of the Church. She is the *aqueduct* of graces, as medieval and modern authors are wont to describe her.

Conjoining these two aspects: the spiritual maternity and the *magisterium* of Mary over the Church, and comparing the teaching of Mother Agreda with that of Vatican II, we are justified in saying that the Council very reasonably reflects in this way on those who dedicate themselves to the general apostolate of the Church: "The Virgin in her life was example for that maternal affection which must animate all those who in the missionary apostolate of the Church cooperate in the

---

or mission of Christ. Without doubt, the Venerable Authoress does not refer to the personal being of her Son, but to His "ministerial being." She cannot participate either the divinity or the humanity of her Son, which is His being. She participates "His being" as Redeemer and as unquestionable Teacher of mankind. She explains this participation via the communication of perfections and corresponding attributes to her new ministry. Mother Agreda attributes to Mary neither juridical nor sacerdotal authority in the Church. She sets Mary "in a new and higher state of knowledge and power," [the order of the hypostatic union. Thus in supplying for Christ as teacher in the Church, she does not substitute for the hierarchy,] but supplies the context for the apostolic teaching. See above in part one, pp. 39-48. [Perhaps the mystery which the Venerable Mother describes here, the key point denied by the Monophysites of old, is best summarized in one phrase by St. Leo the Great: the "consubstantiality" of Christ and His Mother in virtue of the divine Maternity.]

regeneration of men." [152] Where and when did Mary present and show herself as example and model of this "*maternal affection*" so pure and so intense? Was it not precisely during those days when she lived with the Apostles and the primitive Christian communities after the Ascension of the Lord into heaven? Is it really plausible this "maternal affection" could have some other meaning, and be a mere metaphor for something not maternal?…

2) On the basis of what has been set forth here we may affirm that Jesus Christ entrusted to His Mother on the eve of His Ascension into heaven the role of *Teacher of the Church:* of the Apostolic Community and of the communities of the first Christians. This recognition and this concession were a complement of the spiritual maternity, which Jesus himself had proclaimed from the Chair of the Cross.

The Virgin Mary without question and with total commitment and full fidelity fulfilled this responsibility entrusted to her by her Son, if we understand her spiritual maternity in the proper sense, as I think it should be understood.

This vision, which Mother Agreda holds of the image and of the spiritual role of the Virgin Mary in the Church, is perfectly consistent with the *quasi infinite* dignity of the Mother of God, as St. Thomas qualifies it, and with her mission of spiritual Mother as this is presented by the scholastic and speculative mariology and by other authors of her day. In general, until Vatican II, traditional mariology offered a simplified and impoverished vision of Mary in this time of the *historia salutis*. The vision which Mother Agreda offers, the vision of a contemplative soul, is much more objective and enriched. It is, further, more in harmony with the sense in which the Magisterium of the Church has

---

152 Vatican II, *Lumen Gentium*, 65.

understood the spiritual maternity and marian mediation, and in which that Magisterium in our time has also spoken concerning the Mother of the Church.

3)   In addition, the doctrinal teaching which the *MCG* contains on these mysteries of the life of Mary – leaving aside the concrete descriptions and scenic representations typical of the baroque style – is extraordinarily close to the thought of Pope John Paul II, when he explains the role and the "maternal presence" of Mary in the Church, rather than to those impoverished, abbreviated explanations which some ancient theologians and some modern critics offer. [153]

For this very reason I think that this ecclesial vision of the ministry of Mary, which Mother Agreda gives us, is fully consistent, doctrinally, with the teaching of Vatican II. It is a very positive and highly enriched vision of mariology in contrast with what many scholastic mariologies make available to us.

At the present time, there are many mariologists who seek to explore new approaches to the development and progress of mariology. At times they lose their way wandering down paths and pursuing themes of secondary import, such as the study of the historical context in which the life of the Virgin unfolds, and the domestic customs of her times. The perspectives which the doctrine of Mother Agreda opens to our view for the study of the spiritual maternity of Mary and of her magisterium over the Church, of her active presence in the primitive Christian Community, and of her generosity in assisting and in interceding for the disciples of her Son..., are much more positive and assure much more genuine progress for mariology in our time.

4)   Finally, to my way of seeing the matter, this vision of the ministry of Mary, which the Venerable Authoress

---

153 See John Paul II, *RM*, 20-27; 38-47.

gives us in her *MCG*, is very *ecclesial*, and in this context the profoundest and most positive which 17th century Spanish mariology offers us on this theme. [154] This is an unquestionable merit, in addition to many others of the *MCG*, because its doctrine and teaching concerning marian dogma and marian questions, i.e., its mariology, approximates very much that of Vatican II.

From another standpoint Mother Agreda, as a woman and as a consecrated woman, could relate better to the mystery of Mary, and with greater spiritual and human sensitivity, than the over intellectualized and ponderous mariologies of her epoch. Pope John Paul II indicates a reason for this, a reason which finds verification in the Venerable Authoress of the *MCG*, and which is at the same time a reaffirmation of the maternal role of Mary. On Mary and womanhood the Pope significantly observes:

> *This marian dimension of Christian life acquires a special accent in regard to the woman and to her condition. In effect: being feminine bears a singular relation to the Mother of the Redeemer... Here I only wish to set in relief how the figure of Mary of Nazareth throws light on the woman as such, in virtue of fact itself that in the sublime event of the Incarnation of the Son God has engaged the free and active ministry of a woman. For the rest one may affirm that the woman, in admiring Mary, finds in Her the secret for living*

---

154 I refer here only to that aspect of mariology dealing with the relation of Mary to the Church. For if we consider 17th century mariology overall, we must admit that the reflections of scholastic theologians, like José de la Cerda and the Mercedarian S. Saavedra who expound the mystery of Mary in terms of her singular being and her relations with the Most Holy Trinity, are extraordinarily profound.

worthily her femininity and for achieving her true advancement adequately. [155]

The Pope affirms that womanhood holds a *singular relation* with the Mother of the Redeemer. What does this mean, what does this relation involve? Can it be considered as something purely static and lifeless? Or would it not be better to consider this relation as something dynamic, as a predisposition which makes it easier for a woman to understand the mystery of Mary as Mother, and to intuit certain sentiments and dispositions proper to being feminine?

If to these we add the power of grace, which purifies the soul, and the light of that sapiential knowledge communicated during contemplative prayer, a knowledge which enlightens and invigorates the interior faculties of intellect and will, a knowledge with which Mother Agreda was super-endowed as the history of her life proves, we can understand better many passages of the *MCG* without arguing over the sensational and undocumented. Our reflections rest on reasonable proofs and arguments. The doctrine and the attitudes of the mystics, critiqued out of context, have in the greater number of cases always been interpreted negatively as a form of hallucination, error and heresy... But history vindicates them, as we know from the lives of St. Ignatius of Loyola, St. John of Avila, St. Teresa of Jesus and St. John of the Cross, to cite only a few examples of the better known.

5) The "ecclesial note" of the *MCG* appears especially strong at Pentecost, and in the history of the Virgin, when she accompanies St. John to Ephesus, and afterwards returns to Jerusalem, where she gives instructions to the Evangelists. The New Testament guards in silence these events which occurred during this time span. Mother Agreda

---

155 JOHN PAUL II, *RM*, 46.

fills her account with normal and appropriate events. [156] All she affirms, or supposes, is respectful and accords with the figure of the Mother of God, with the silence of the Bible and with the normal unfolding of the life of the primitive Church. [157]

In conclusion: her teachings and basic affirmations concerning the spiritual maternity and the magisterium of the Virgin Mary over the Apostles and the primitive Christian communities, from the doctrinal standpoint and as "*ecclesial note*" of the *MCG*, find their echo in the mariological environment of our time, nourished on the doctrine of Vatican II and the papal Magisterium.

Lastly, I do not believe we are guilty of equivocation, when we claim that the *Mystical City of God* by the Venerable Mother Mary of Jesus of Agreda is a marian work of highest caliber – notwithstanding disputes over the historical character of marginal facts which she introduces – in so far as among works composed by 17th century Spanish theologians

---

156 The account of these facts fills part 3 of the *MCG*, Books VII and VIII, pp. 1109-1181; 1299-1458 [IV, 29-619]. Multiple assertions can be found in which the Venerable Authoress accents the spiritual and magisterial work which Mary accomplished in the Church: "The Lord granted her the highest gifts to work in the Church" (p. 1123 [IV, n. 4, 32]), etc. The historical facts, as propounded by the Authoress, can be separated from the doctrine, or teaching (although the teaching ultimately rests on the revealed history of the New Testament). The facts in question here contain nothing in themselves contrary to documented history, even if a few of those recounted include rather surprising facts. This technique was part of the religious and devotional style of the time in explaining doctrine truly revealed, but easy to overlook without such concrete depiction.

157 The greater number of facts to which the Venerable Authoress refers in this third part do not enjoy great historical worth beyond that of their probability or validity as hypotheses. A hypothesis, however, should not be rejected, merely because it is a hypothesis rather than proven fact, for on occasion it can be a legitimate instrument of study, indeed of scientific study. At times it can open a path to follow in describing the truth, especially when such description entails obscure facts lacking documentation.

the *MCG* sets in relief with greater detail, objectivity and liveliness the "*ecclesial note*" of mariology.

4. The *Mystical City of God* and the Biblical "Note-orientation"

a. *The biblical note-orientation*

The note, or *biblical orientation*, as Pope Paul VI calls it, is also a postulate and a need of marian devotion, and by extension also of mariology, as sign of authenticity. Thus Paul VI proposes it, taking his inspiration from Vatican II. [158]

On the other hand, when we turn our attention primarily to mariology, we find that the Council itself recommends to priests the study of Sacred Scripture with special care, for the Word of God must be the "soul" of theology. [159]

Vatican II itself has followed this norm in the redaction of the marian chapter of the Constitution on the Church, no. 55, dealing with "*the Mother of the Messiah in the Old Testament*," preceded by some general considerations in prior numbers, provides an exordium or preliminary sketch of the guidelines governing the rest of the chapter, no. 56-59, where the Virgin in the New Testament is treated.

Besides this, the Council lays down a number of principles which we also find applied in the *MCG*, principles which served the Venerable Authoress in properly structuring the entire work. Here is an example in point from the Council, which states: "*The books of the Old Testament narrate the history of salvation... These first documents, as they are read in the Church, and as they are interpreted in the light of a further*

---

[158] Paul VI proposes this orientation "following the path traced out by the Council teachings" (PAUL VI, *MC*, 29-30); he cites as source for his inspiration Vatican II, *Lumen Gentium*, 66-69. However, nos. 55-56 must also be taken account of.

[159] Vatican II, *Optatam totius*, 16 and *Dei Verbum*, 24, respectively.

and fuller revelation, reveal little by little...the figure of the woman, Mother of the Redeemer." [160]

All Scripture for the rest, both the Old and the New Testament, *"at each step manifests with greater clarity the role of the Mother of the Savior in the economy of salvation."* [161] This same point is made by Paul VI in the form of an axiom:

> *The Bible, in proposing so admirably God's design for the salvation of mankind, is totally permeated by the mystery of the Savior, and so contains, from Genesis to the Apocalypse, unquestionable references to Her who was Mother and Associate of the Savior.* [162]

b. *The biblical "note-orientation" in the* Mystical City of God

1) The fact is that Mother Agreda composed the *MCG*, fully conscious and convinced of these principles, in our day formulated by the Magisterium of the Church. These principles are rooted in and find their basis in the Word of God itself: in the time of promise of the Messiah and in the time of fulfillment of those promises. [163]

For Mother Agreda the entire Bible has a marian meaning; all of it, taken as a whole, refers to the Mother of the Redeemer Messiah. This is because she also understands that the Bible *"proposes the design of God for the salvation of mankind."* And Mother Agreda teaches that from the Virgin Mother's origin, from her predestination in the eternal designs of God, and from the very start of creation, Mary has been associated with the Redeemer, as His collaborator

---

160 Vatican II, *Lumen Gentium*, 55.

161 Vatican II, *Lumen Gentium*, 55.

162 PAUL VI, *MC*, 30.

163 See principally: Lk 4:16-21; 24:25-27; Jn 2:18-22; 8:56-59; 1 Cor 10:4.

in the work of redemption. In her view of the mystery of Mary, the Mother of God is in the Bible ever present, entirely united to the mystery of her Redeemer Son. To take account of this with greater clarity, it suffices to consider the title of chapter 11 of Book One in the first part of the *MCG: That in the creation of all things the Lord had in mind Christ, our Lord, and His Most Holy Mother.* [164] With this criterion and along these lines Mother Agreda expounds the christological and marian interpretation of chapter 8 of Proverbs and chapter 12 of the Apocalypse. [165]

I do not know whether as a consequence of this biblical interpretation or as root and source of it, Christ and Mary constitute a *moral, mystical unity* in the work of redemption: Jesus Christ as Redeemer and absolute Savior, Mary as collaborator with Him in due proportion; a *mystical unity* as Mother and Son, who share a same nature and a same mission. For this reason the entire Scripture, which is the history of salvation, mirrors and is referred to the Son of God, Redeemer, and to His Mother, His collaborator in the redemption.

2)   Hence, it comes about that the *MCG* is a biblical-theological and a spiritual elaboration of the mysteries of Mary, relative to the mysteries of the life of Jesus. With all the more reason, a properly called *"history" of the Life of the Virgin* in the hands of Mother Agreda becomes at once an interpretation of those biblical texts, which are the source of her knowledge, and a biblically permeated exposition of the dogmas and relative truths touching the Most Holy Virgin.

---

164 *MCG*, Lib. I, ch. 11, pp. 71-79 [I, 125-140].

165 *MCG*, ch. 5-7, pp. 37-54 [I, 62-92]; and ch, 8-10, pp. 54-71 [I, 93-124]. We have already set out in the first part of our study the approach of Mother Agreda on this point, and the structure which she gives her work. In order not to prolong the explanation here or to repeat themes already commented upon, we refer the reader to what we have written above.

She is conversant with theological theories governing the formulation of marian truths, and is familiar with the various senses of the Word of God. These she applies in her interpretations, selecting whichever is the more appropriate for the case at hand: literal sense, or *according to the letter*, spiritual sense, mystical sense, symbolic sense, and transcendent sense. This occasionally applies to the Mother of God by reason of her singular dignity, quasi-infinite.

Mother Agreda interprets the marian chapters of the Old and New Testament, not according to the laws of scientific and philological exegesis, but in the light which the Lord had given her from her youth, [166] and which he especially communicated to her in contemplative prayer at the time of composing her marian work. For this reason she generally employs in her interpretations the mystical and spiritual senses, to which, based on his own experience, St. John of the Cross alludes in his "Introduction" to the *Spiritual Canticle*. In the composition of her work, Mother Agreda considers as teachers and interlocutors God and the Virgin Mary herself.

From this standpoint the *MCG* is one of the more important 17th century works of marian theology. It interprets a number of chapters of the Bible, which might be read otherwise, in a mariological sense. Some commentators on the *Canticle of Canticles* (A. Hurtado de Mendoza and M. del Rio, and others of the 17th century), composed works of merit from the standpoint of scientific and philological exegesis. Hence, their works were redacted in another style and with other objectives. The *MCG* followed different guidelines. And in this it is one of the most important works of its kind. Its true soul is the Bible, both as regards its content and as regards the magisterial lines of its structure. Along

---

166 See *MCG*, Lib. I, ch. 5: "Of the intelligence of Sacred Scripture which the Most High gave me," pp. 37 ff.

such lines a number of specialized scholars in our times have commented. [167]

It is surprising that in the *MCG* there is not found a single error, and the Authoress has not proposed a single false or unbalanced interpretation of the Bible. Given that she had no particular scholarly training in these areas, nor any special preparation for exegetical work, this is not only surprising but also astounding. All her interpretations of various and numerous biblical texts fit neatly within one or another of the different senses which the great masters: theologians, exegetes and mystics, recognize as valid in Catholic interpretation of the Word of God.

In this the *MCG* enjoys a double merit. On the one hand, the Bible is a basic determinant of its doctrinal content, fully permeated by its spirit. On the other hand, this work is outstanding for the variety and richness of the biblical senses which Mother Agreda utilizes, and above all for correctness in and for the theological and spiritual wisdom guiding her interpretation of so large a number of texts from the Sacred Books, an achievement fully in the style of the great Spanish mystical and spiritual masters of the 16th and 17th centuries.

---

167 In this regard see in particular: A. Artola, *La Venerable Madre Maria de Jesús de Agreda*, Agreda 2002, n. 4; L. Diez Merino, *Empleo de la Biblia en la "Mística Ciudad de Dios" de Sor María de Agreda*, in *Estudios Marianos* LXIX (2003), pp. 81-110.

PART THREE:

CONCLUSIONS

From what has been so far expounded, one can draw various important conclusions: some relative to Mother Agreda and her work, the *Mystical City of God*, both from the standpoint of content and of structure; others, with relation to the *Mystical City of God* and its present relevance:

1) The image which the *MCG* gives us of the Virgin Mary, Mother of the Son of God and collaborator with Him in the work of redemption, is the gospel image handed down to us by the Magisterium of the Church, one depicted with the help of insights which theology and the ecclesial tradition have attained across the centuries. It is an image which in fundamentals is in no way in **contrast** with the biblical image.

2) The mariology of the *MCG* contains no theological error; to the contrary it makes a positive contribution to the theological explanation of the marian dogmas and the fundamental truths of Catholic mariology. As to its structure and historico-narrative character as well as its doctrinal content, not only is the *MCG* compatible with the mariology of Vatican II, but also in notable matters it coincides with this Council's teachings, both in structure and in terminology, as well as in doctrine and in its fundamental orientation.

3) To interpret correctly the *Mystical City of God* one must take precise account of this hermeneutical key, viz., that one is dealing here with a "history" of the life of the Blessed Virgin in the broad sense of the term history, with hagiography composed in the heart of the baroque epoch, when embellishments enjoyed a certain precedent over pure history, and when sensational events were knowingly employed to set in relief and exalt the dignity and noble qualities of the

protagonists. History was written and embellished in view of the exemplarity of the Saints, not in order to meet the criteria of rigorous, critical history.

4) The facts and affirmations presented in the *Mystical City of God* as "historical facts" in the life of Mary are not really errors in the strict sense. In the absence of historical documentation they should be considered, at the very least, as probable facts, which could very well have happened as presented. One might object that the *MCG* abuses "*miraculous sensationalism*" in regard to Mary. Even with this one must take account of the fact, 1) that as Mother of God she is a *singular and unique Member*, therefore in a sense "sensational" figure in the history of salvation, where she *occupies the highest place after Christ* in this history, as Vatican II teaches; [168] and further 2) recognize that we do not know the limits of the designs of the Triune God in her regard, and that we do not know in what measure graces were bestowed on her and 3) admit that she was enriched with such "sensational" gifts, given that she possesses a *quasi-infinite dignity*, as mariologists following in the footsteps of St. Thomas generally teach. [169]

5) In regard to the biography of Mother Agreda there is no doubt that the greater part of the information which it provides concerning the Virgin Mary, and which constitutes the fundamental content of the *Mystical City of God*, is fruit of contemplative prayer, not of study. These were graces which we may class as

---

[168] Vatican II, *Lumen Gentium*, 53-54.

[169] *Summa Theologica*, I, q. 25, a. 6, ad 6: "In so far as she is Mother of God, Mary possesses a *quasi*-infinite dignity in her relations with God, infinite goodness; and under this aspect nothing greater is possible, as it is not impossible to find anything which is greater than God himself."

"illuminations," ordinary and extraordinary, "interior locutions," like those received by other Saints.[170] She expounds with considerable prolixity and describes in detail the mysteries of the Virgin, because in the baroque epoch in which she lived embellishment enjoyed priority over simple or merely factual statement of the truth. Embellishment, however, is not a synonym for falsification or invention of facts.

---

170 Similar locutions, although in a more sober and moderate style, are found in St. Teresa of Jesus, as is evident from the testimony of her *Life* (ch. 26, 6), and of her *Cases of Conscience*, where she states, for example: *"The Lord taught me a way of prayer"* (Cta. 2, 2); or *"There are so many (things) which I see (during prayer), and what I understand of the great works of God, and how he has guided all of them..."* (Cta. 3, 11). See the *Cuentas de Conciencia*, 7, 8, 10, 11, 12, 13, 17, 19, 20, 22, 25, 26, etc., in St. Teresa, *Obras Completas*, Madrid 2000. To cite another example, from the biography of St. Alonso de Orozco, it appears that while he was in the convent of Seville, he received an "inspiration" or interior locution of the All Holy Virgin, that he should write or put in writing his interior experiences. And no one finds fault with these phenomena or calls their truth in question.

A DESIDERATUM

1) In view of what I have expounded in this essay, I make bold to petition the Hierarchy of the Church or "whomsoever it concerns," that the figure of Mother Mary of Jesus of Agreda be rehabilitated in the Church, that the *nihil obstat* be conceded, and that the process of beatification be permitted to proceed freely in proper form and according to the established norms.

This is not merely a personal desire. It is also a *desideratum* of all who know the true doctrine and the mariological teachings of the *Mystical City of God*, interpreted according to the signs of the times. I am perfectly aware that not all mariologists are of this opinion. Nonetheless, I think that their attitude betrays in some way a certain ignorance of objective truth, or an interpretation of the mariology of the *Mystical City of God* according to out-dated criteria, which on the basis of arguments set forth here, lack solid grounds.

Moreover, in our days a number of more or less questionable figures, much discussed in the history of the Church and of theology, have been rehabilitated, for example: Galileo, Martin Luther, Antonio Rosmini… It is not my purpose here to find fault, even minimal, with the rehabilitation of these persons or insinuate judgment on their persons. But precisely in view of their rehabilitation (despite legitimate grounds in some cases for questioning this) and in view of the facts adduced in this study, one cannot help but experience considerable shock over the conduct of the Church in regard to the Venerable Mary of Jesus of Agreda. It seems a contradiction – to some it might seem an "unjustifiable discrimination" – to have annulled the condemnations in the aforementioned cases, and to continue in the bosom of the Church this opposition to the Cause of Mother Agreda. For some good Christians, to maintain such an attitude is comparably the equivalent of insult, an attitude not easy to justify in our times.

2) On the other hand, maintenance of the *censure* against the *Mystical City of God* and the marginalization following upon it as logical consequence, harmful both to the person and to the work of the Venerable Mother Agreda, in great part deprives the Church, the theologians and the people of God of that enlightenment from a doctrine whose circulation could contribute decisively to the advancement of mariology, and to the renewal and realization of marian piety and spirituality.

Thus an injustice is brought about, and the Church is deprived of a blessing. The Church in our days is much in need of just that blessing, testimonies to a life of faith doubling as efficacious stimuli to the same, such as that of Mother Agreda, and of works like hers illustrating the faith of the people of God, in a manner attractive and accessible to all, via the *way of beauty*, as Pope Paul VI termed it, which is the way followed and taught by the *Mystical City of God*.

3) Today, when the Church has asked pardon on various occasions – via the voice of His Holiness, the late Pope John Paul II – for various errors committed throughout history, it seems a senseless and unjustifiable anachronism to maintain these censures and this internal conflict, one that never should have arisen, against the Venerable Mother Agreda and against her work: the *Mystical City of God*, and one that has impeded the course of her Cause for beatification. Her rehabilitation would be a rejection and a definitive correction of past errors. This would also, as I see it, at the same time turn out to be a great gift and outstanding service highly beneficial to the Church.

4)   Finally, the Venerable Mother Agreda in her *Mystical City of God* gave written formulation to certain intuitions and initiated a number of theological reflections which in the course of time the Magisterium of the Church has elevated to the status of dogmas of faith or of doctrines universally acknowledged in the Catholic Church. As examples one may cite her defense of the Immaculate Conception, and her teaching on the Virgin Mary, *Mother of the Church and Teacher of the Apostles.*

This came about in virtue of the harmonious development of the marian dogmas and of the truths which are contained in the Word of God and in the tradition of the Church, either explicitly or implicitly.

The Immaculate Conception of Mary, preserved from contracting original sin in virtue of the merits of her Redeemer Son, and the divine Maternity itself, which at the same time is a soteriological Maternity, are two characteristic dogmas, in whose explanation the knowledge and sapiential science of the Authoress, who received extraordinary light in the loving contemplation of these mysteries, is outstanding. Thanks to this light she could enjoy an exceptional in-depth knowledge of the mystery of Christ the Redeemer, and of the role of His Mother in the history of salvation. This is the key to the reading of the *MCG* and to the interpretation of its doctrine.

The progress of the Cause of Mother Agreda poses a question, which after more than three centuries hopefully will find an answer. In view of the facts, and in particular in view of the mariology of the *MCG*, the reply should be entirely favorable to the Venerable Authoress. The facts, which we have expounded in this essay, annul the validity of the censures, and silence the accusations which hitherto have torpedoed the course of her Cause for beatification.

The *Mystical City of God* is a compendium of mariology, in its basic content and in its magisterial lines, compatible with the mariology of Vatican II. In virtue of this profound compatibility, the mariology of the *MCG*, which in our times has been for its accusers motive and heart of stubborn opposition to the Cause of the Venerable Mother, in fact has turned out to be the best and strongest guarantee of its objectivity and truth.

Biographical Sketch
of Ven. Mother Agreda

During the year 2002 the fourth centenary of the birth of the Venerable Mary of Jesus of Agreda, one of the most remarkable figures of 17th century Spanish mariology and of the spiritual literature of the baroque age, was solemnly celebrated.

She was born the 2nd of April, 1602 in the city of Agreda (Soria), the "city of three cultures" on the frontier of Castille and Aragon. The city of Agreda then belonged to the Diocese of Tarazona, whose Bishop at that time was Diego de Yepes, friend and confessor of St. Teresa of Jesus and counselor of Philip II. At the age of 16 years, with her mother and a sister, she entered the Order of the Immaculate Conception (Conceptionist Franciscan Poor Clares), founded by St. Beatrice of Silva, converting their own dwelling into a monastery. She was a woman highly endowed *with extraordinary human gifts* (M. Hernández Sánchez-Barba). She in fact was foundress of the present Conceptionist monastery in Agreda. At the age of 25 she was chosen superioress of the Community. She wrote various treatises on the spiritual life, some of which have never been published. Her most important work is the *Mystical City of God.* Its title has symbolic meaning and designates the Virgin Mary, Mother of the Son of God, as city, temple, tabernacle of the Godhead. This work is an authentic compendium of mariology, written between 1655-1660, in the form of a history of the life of Our Lady. Sr. Mary of Jesus died, the 24th of May, 1665, Pentecost Sunday.

Sr. Mary of Jesus was friend and counselor of Philip IV both in matters spiritual and in questions of government, and enjoyed an extensive correspondence with this King of Spain. This correspondence is a first class source for coming to know and evaluate her virtues, her human and supernatural qualities and gifts.

She appears to have enjoyed the gift of bilocation and acted as missionary to the natives of New Mexico and Texas between 1620-1631, an activity documented in the process carried out for her beatification. Like other great figures in the history of theology and spirituality during the 16th and 17th centuries, such as St. Ignatius of Loyola, St. Teresa of Jesus, St. John of the Cross, St. John of Avila, Fray Luis of Leon...the Venerable Mary of Jesus was also accused before the Spanish Inquisition which carried out a number of measures designed to investigate her spirit and teaching. In 1696 the University of Paris published a severe and disgraceful censure of the *Mystical City of God*, lacking in objectivity, which torpedoed the cause of the Venerable, and has interrupted its normal course to the present day. Today many persons work for her rehabilitation with the same interest which was present in her enthusiastic admirers of the 17th and subsequent centuries. The historian, M. Hernández Sánchez-Barba considers Mother Agreda as *the most interesting spiritual figure of 17th century Spain.*

Further reading on Mother Agreda:

Sor María de Jesús de Agreda, *Mística Ciudad de Dios. Vida de María*, ed. Celestino Salaguren, OFM. Madrid 1970 (reprinted 1982). Pp. 1509 (critical Spanish edition). English translation: *The Mystical City of God. The Divine History and Life of the Virgin*, ed. Fiscar Marison (= Rev. George J. Blatter). Chicago 1912, reissued Wheeling, W.V. 1949; Washington, N.J. 1971. 3 parts in 4 vols.

Italian translation: *Mistica Città di Dio. Vita della Vergine Madre di Dio*. Assisi 2000. Pp. 1109.

Manuel Peña García, *Sor María de Jesús de Agreda*. Agreda 1997. Pp. 358.

Angel Martínez Moñux, *María, Mística Ciudad de Dios. Una mariología interactiva*. Burgos 2001. Pp. 418.

Aa.Vv., *La Madre Agreda, una mujer del siglo XXI:* Universidad Internacional Alfonso VIII, Monografías Universitarias, 15. Soria 2000. Pp. 279.

Aa.Vv., *El papel de Sor María de Jesús de Agreda en el Barroco español:* Universidad Internacional Alfonso VIII, Monografías Universitarias, 13. Soria 2002. Pp. 263.

Spanish Mariological Society, *La Madre Agreda y la mariología española del siglo XVII: Estudios Marianos LXIX*. Salamanca 2003. Pp. 431.

THE ACADEMY OF THE IMMACULATE

The Academy of the Immaculate, founded in 1992, is inspired by and based on a project of St. Maximilian M. Kolbe (never realized by the Saint because of his death by martyrdom at the age of 47, August 14, 1941). Among its goals the Academy seeks to promote at every level the study of the Mystery of the Immaculate Conception and the universal maternal mediation of the Virgin Mother of God, and to sponsor publication and dissemination of the fruits of this research in every way possible.

The Academy of the Immaculate is a non-profit religious-charitable organization of the Roman Catholic Church, incorporated under the laws of the Commonwealth of Massachusetts, with its central office at Our Lady's Chapel, POB 3003, New Bedford, MA 02741-3003.

A Selection of Books from the Academy of the Immaculate

All Generations Shall Call Me Blessed *by Fr. Stefano Manelli, FI* A scholarly, easy to read book tracing Mary's role in the Old Testament through prophecies, figures, and symbols to Mary's presence in the New Testament. A concise exposition which shows clearly Mary's place in the economy of Salvation.

A Month with Mary *Daily Meditations for a Profound reform of the heart in the School of Mary* *by Don Dolindo Ruotolo* This little book was written by a holy Italian priest Father Dolondo Ruotolo (1882-1970). Originally written as spiritual thoughts to his spiritual daughter, the work is comprised of thirty-one meditations for the month of May. The month of Mary is the month of *a profound reform of heart:* we must leave ourselves and adorn ourselves with every virtue and every spiritual good.

Jesus Our Eucharistic Love *by Fr. Stefano Manelli, FI* A treasure of Eucharistic devotional writings and examples from the Saints showing their stirring Eucharistic love and devotion. A valuable aid for reading meditatively before the Blessed Sacrament.

Virgo Facta Ecclesia *by Franciscan Friars of the Immaculate* is made up of two parts: the first a biography on St. Francis of Assisi and the second part on the marian character of the Franciscan Order based on its long marian tradition, from St. Francis to St. Maximilian Kolbe.

Not Made by Hands *by Thomas Sennott* An excellent resource book covering the two most controversial images in existence: the Holy Image of Our Lady of Guadalupe on the tilma of Juan Diego and the Sacred Image of the Crucified on the Shroud of Turin, giving scientific evidence for their authenticity and exposing the fraudulent carbon 14 test.

Do You Know Our Lady *by Rev. Mother Francesca Perillo, FI* This handy treatise (125 pages) covers the many rich references to Mary, as prefigured in the Old Testament women and prophecies and as found in the New Testament from the Annunciation to Pentecost. Mary's role is seen ever beside her Divine Son, and the author shows how scripture supports Mary's role as Mediatrix of all Graces. Though scripture scholars can read it with profit, it is an easy read for everyone. Every marian devotee should have a copy for quick reference.

For the Life of the World *by Jerzy Domanski, OFM Conv.* The former international director of the Knights of the Immaculata and Guardian of the City of the Immaculate in Poland examines Fr. Kolbe's Eucharistic, spiritual life as a priest and adorer of the Eucharist, all in the context of his love of the Immaculate.

Devotion to Our Lady *by Fr. Stefano M. Manelli, FI* This book is a must for all those who desire to know the beauty and value of marian devotion and want to increase their fervent love towards their heavenly Mother. Since it draws abundantly from the examples and writings of the Saints, it offers the devotee a very concrete and practical aid for living out a truly marian life.

Mary at the Foot of the Cross I *Acts of the International Symposium on Mary, Coredemptress, Mediatrix and Advocate.* This over 400 page book on a week-long symposium held in 2000 at Ratcliffe College in England, has a whole array of outstanding mariologists from many parts of the world. To name a few: Bishop Paul Hnilica; Fr. Bertrand De Margerie, SJ; Dr. Mark Miravalle; Fr. Stefano Manelli, FI; Fr. Aidan Nichols, OP; Msgr. Arthur Calkins; and Fr. Peter Fehlner, FI who was the moderator. Ask about books on similar symposiums in 2001-2005.

Who is Mary? *Fr. Gabriele M. Pellettieri, FI* This book is a concise marian catechism presented in a question/answer format. In this little work of love and scholarship the sweet mystery of Mary is unveiled in all its beauty and simplicity. It is a very helpful resource both for those who want to know the truth about Mary and those who want to instruct others.

Padre Pio of Pietrelcina *by Fr. Stefano Manelli, FI* This 144 page popular life of Padre Pio is packed with details about his life, spirituality, and charisms, by one who knew the Padre intimately. The author turned to Padre Pio for guidance in establishing a new Community, the Franciscans of the Immaculate.

Come Follow Me *by Fr. Stefano Manelli, FI* A book directed to any young person contemplating a Religious vocation. Informative, with many inspiring illustrations and words from the lives and writings of the Saints on the challenging vocation of total dedication in the following of Christ and His Immaculate Mother through the three vows of religion.

A Primer on the Absolute Primacy of Christ *Blessed John Duns Scotus and the Franciscan Thesis* *by Fr. Maximilian Mary Dean, FI* Every disputed question in current theology begins or ends with some reference to christocentrism or the primacy of Christ, but rarely provides any clear definition of these terms, and even more rarely makes reference to the theologian, Bl. John Duns Scotus, who was most responsible for the key to the correct understanding and use of this terminology. Here, for the first time in over half a century, in an English style accessible to the non-professional reader, we have an accurate detailed account of Scotus' explanation of this core theme on Christian thought, traditionally dubbed the Franciscan thesis, or the absolute, joint predestination of Jesus and Mary to be King and Queen of the universe.

Saints And Marian Shrine Series
Edited by Bro. Francis Mary, FI

A Handbook on Guadalupe This well researched book on Guadalupe contains 40 topical chapters by leading experts on Guadalupe with new insights and the latest scientific findings. A number of chapters deal with Our Lady's role as the patroness of the pro-life movement. Well illustrated.

St. Thérèse: Doctor of the Little Way A compendium of 32 chapters covering many unique facets about the latest Doctor of the Church by 23 authors including Fr. John Hardon, SJ; Msgr. Vernon Johnson; Sister Marie of the Trinity, OCD; Stephanè Piat. This different approach to St. Thérèse is well illustrated.

Marian Shrines of France The four major marian shrines and apparitions of France during the 19th century: Our Lady at Rue du Bac, Paris (Miraculous Medal); La Salette; Lourdes and Pontmain shows how in the 19th century — Our Lady was checkmating our secular, Godless 20th century, introducing the present Age of Mary. Well illustrated with many color pictures.

Padre Pio - The Wonder Worker The latest on this popular saint of our times including the two inspirational homilies given by Pope John Paul II during the beatification celebration in Rome. The first part of the book is a short biography. The second is on his spirituality, charisms, apostolate of the confessional, and his great works of charity.

Marian Shrines of Italy Another in the series of "Marian Saints and Shrines," with 36 pages of colorful illustrations on over thirty of the 1500 marian shrines in Italy. The book covers that topic with an underlying theme of the intimate and vital relationship between Mary and the Church. This is especially apparent in Catholic Italy, where the center of the Catholic Faith is found.

Kolbe *Saint of the Immaculata* Of all the books in the Marian Saints and Shrines series, this one is the most controversial and thus the most needed in order to do justice to the Saint, whom Pope John Paul II spoke of as "the Saint of our difficult century [twentieth]." Is it true, as reported in a PBS documentary, that the Saint was anti-Semitic? What is the reason behind misrepresenting this great modern day Saint? Is a famous mariologist right in accusing the Saint of being in error by holding that Mary is the Mediatrix of all Graces? The book has over 35 chapters by over ten authors, giving an in-depth view of one of the greatest marian Saints of all times.

For a complete listing of books, tapes and CD's from the Academy of the Immaculate please refer to our catalog. Request a free catalog by email, letter, or phone via the contact information given below for the Academy of the Immaculate.

Special rates are available with 25% to 50% discount depending on the number of books, plus postage. For ordering books and further information on rates to book stores, schools and parishes: **Academy of the Immaculate**, *164 Charleston Ridge Dr., Mocksville, NC 27028, Phone/FAX (336) 751-2990, E-mail Mimike@pipeline.com. Quotations on bulk rates shipped directly by the box from the printery, contact: Franciscans of the Immaculate, P.O. Box 3003, New Bedford, MA 02741, (508) 996-8274, FAX (508) 996-8296, E-mail: ffi@marymediatrix. com. Website: www.marymediatrix.com.*